A Field Guide to Advanced Spiritual Warfare

DELIVERANCE, EXORCISM, AND HEALING
THE EFFECTS OF RITUAL ABUSE

PASTORAL CARE FOR THE SPIRITUALLY
AFFLICTED SOUL

Michael J. Norton

Michael J. Norton Press
SAN FRANCISCO, CA

A Field Guide to Advanced Spiritual Warfare - Deliverance, Exorcism, and Healing the Effects of Ritual Abuse Michael J. Norton. —1st ed.

ISBN-10: 0-692-88992-2

ISBN-13: 978-0-692-88992-3

Library of Congress Cataloging-in-Publication Data is on file at the Library of Congress, Washington, D.C.

Contents

Dedications

To my wife Lisa, for standing by me during the wraths of warfare and truly understanding the victory at the cross. I am blessed through you. You are the Proverbs 31 wife. Thank you for the awesome book cover design!

To Toni Taigen for being a mentor and a powerful ministry friend in working with shattered lives. For making me a part of In the Potter's Hands I am truly grateful.

To Adrienne Powell for your unshakeable spiritual zeal and being the one who rides shotgun on the dark ministry calls. I wouldn't think of calling anyone else for warfare.

To Mark Neitz for being my ongoing ministry mentor and for keeping me in mind when it comes to overseas spiritual warfare.

To Pastor Jimi Merrell for being a lifelong friend and brother in Christ. You had the vision back in 2008 to produce field guides for ministers.

To Andrea Norton for your time in assisting me in both this project and in ministry.

To the survivors of severe trauma at In the Potter's Hands

You can judge anything in the world by this. God builds up and the Devil tears down.

- Lester Sumrall

Pastoral Care is defective unless it can deal thoroughly with the evils we have suffered as well as with the sins we have committed.

- Frank Lake, Clinical Theology

Preface

The M16 Ministries, *A Field Guide to Advanced Spiritual Warfare*, will guide you through some of your toughest ministry cases involving spiritual warfare and complicated inner healing. This field guide is intended for pastors, clergy, Christian counselors, and lay people who who provided pastoral care to souls in deep spiritual bondage. The Christian media is overflowing with books and training on the subject matter of low-level demonic deliverance. Some churches and ministries have built corporate empires around specialized training and media. Much of the material provided in these environments is growing dangerously more towards a *new gnosis*[1], than being effective in spiritual warfare and inner healing. These new approaches to ministry are popular because they are process oriented. The process-based ministry is favorable for producing teaching materials and classes. Sadly, this form of ministry falls short when it comes to healing ministry for souls with spiritual afflictions. The downfall to this approach is that it's human doctrine trying to bring healing to the spiritually afflicted soul (oppressed soul). Through these popular methodologies, souls seldom receive true healing. When the minister employs doctrinal healing (man's knowledge in place of God's providence) we tend to see a lot of people come out of the ministry session in worse shape than when they first walked in. It is Jesus alone that heals souls.

All healings are unique. For this reason we can't formulate a process on how to heal afflicted souls. The number one thing to remember is that Jesus heals souls and not us. When providing prayer ministry you must

---

1   Gnosis – knowledge of spiritual mysteries that is derived through experience.

be in step with what Jesus is doing and give yourself the freedom to know you don't have the answers for what He will do to bring about the healing. You must also release yourself from any timeframe or agenda in healing.

I would like to give a case example of an afflicted soul that represents the dangers of process based ministry. One young woman came to counseling, named Sarah, who was at wit's end with her life-long, daily struggle. Whenever she became frustrated her mind would make her do these crazy mental puzzles in her head she had to solve or else be tormented. Sarah's family took her to several large church institutions that provide inner healing ministry called, Sozo prayer. Sozo prayer (meaning "deliver" in Greek) is a popular inner healing and deliverance ministry that is in many charismatic churches. During Sarah's prayer session, some of her multiple identities were triggered and surfaced to speak with the three members of the Sozo prayer team. The prayer team immediately jumped to the wrong conclusion that Sarah's fragmented human parts[2] were demonic spirits. By judging from what they were physically seeing, and not relying on the gifts of the Holy Spirit, they concluded that they were dealing with demons. This scenario has surfaced far too many times now with the people we counsel for inner healing.

Because the ministers couldn't cast out the fractured human parts, they thought they were dealing with powerful demons. It stirred such a hysteria among the prayer team that they felt it necessary to get Sozo-ed themselves and have the demonic spirits removed from them. From Sarah's own horrible firsthand experience, she left the session believing that she was demon possessed. Sarah was now worse off than when she entered the prayer session. This incident wasn't the first-time Sarah had went to a Sozo prayer session for healing. She had participated multiple times, but each time her condition would get worse. Sarah really didn't want to go to any Sozo sessions, her over zealous Christian friends were hoping for a miraculous prayer bullet to heal Sarah's fractured condition, and pressured her to attend. Even though her friends were convinced of an instant healing, the more times Sarah went and received no heal-

---

2 Fractured human parts - dissociative identity disorder. Multiple identities created from severe childhood trauma.

ing, the more her parts and her core self started believing that God had forsaken her and turned her over to her tormentors. Since Sarah's will was compromised she couldn't tell her pushy friends, "No!" So they would stop taking her to these prayer sessions that weren't helping her at all. Sarah even went to a very popular church in my area that operates in Sozo prayer, where her parts were angry and refused to cooperate with the lead prayer minister. This lead prayer minister thought she was dealing with angry demons and told Sarah that she believed she would never heal. The poorly trained minister threw the guilt trip of harboring unforgiveness on this fractured soul as the reason for not receiving her healing. Sarah was now struggling with horrible thoughts of suicide.

Many ill-fated Sozos later, one of Sarah's very close friends, who was also a friend of mine, suggested that she go to a little counseling office and seek deliverance ministry. The repeated bad ministry experience programmed Sarah into believing her identities were demons. She warned us of the nasty demons inside of her, saying that we would freak out like the Sozo ministers from previous prayer sessions. Within the first couple of minutes, her parts came up and started interacting with us during the counseling session. My prayer team and I evaluated that Sarah's problem wasn't demonic possession. We were dealing with fractured children identities. We were able to get to work almost immediately in identifying the switching[3] fractured souls. What our team observed from the first session was that Sarah's core presenter had no control over her free will. Another very young and angry child part of her controlled her free will. For some reason, this part held control and felt it necessary to constantly punish and torment the rest of the soul by forcing them to carry out strange meaningless tasks. The goal of the mind games was to enforce self-hatred.

After several sessions, our ministry team could identify that the root of Sarah's dissociation was Christian ritual abuse. Her mother was very doctrinal to Sarah when she was growing up. There were a lot of detach-

---

3 Switching – the changing of internal identity to another in a soul with multiple identities.

ment issues with mom and a very unhealthy childhood. Whenever Sarah did something wrong in her house, her mom would make her do chores; not normal chores, but chores selected by a wounded and obsessive compulsive mother with poor foundations in her faith. At a very young age, Sarah's mom programmed into her mind that she was an unforgiving child. And unforgiving children go to hell. Sarah grew up in a Christian home with the twisted message that Jesus didn't love her. This unnerving combination of the mother's controlling nature, obsessive compulsiveness and false doctrines of Jesus became a dissociated prison of Sarah's soul. This sort of inner healing takes lots of time. We're making slow, but steady progress with Sarah. The greatest hurdle has been the false Jesus deprogramming and introducing her to the true Jesus. We're still dealing with Sarah's wounds from the poor ministry of the inner healing teams. This left soul wounds that are slowly healing in Sarah.

What I addressed here is a common problem with rapidly emerging Christian charismatic inner healing and deliverance ministries. You're probably wondering, "How did your counseling and prayer team catch the fact that Sarah had human parts and the other prayer teams didn't? Why didn't a minister of exorcism seek the route of casting out demons from Sarah? How did you know what to do?" It's simple. We fully surrendered to what Jesus wanted to do in the prayer session. When the afflicted soul comes to us for help, we don't have a clue as to the depths of the damage of the heart and soul. We only understand one thing, and that is the fact that Jesus is going to heal the broken heart and the afflicted soul, whether tormented, fractured, or even possessed.

Sarah and many other souls like her are the reason I wrote the M16 Ministries: *A Field Guide to Advanced Spiritual Warfare*. I pray that this guide helps get you over some ministry hurdles, and makes you aware of the different types of afflicted souls you may encounter and how to help them. I will also fill in the blanks as to the differences in deliverance ministry and exorcism. As our Catholic friends already know, yes, there is a difference. But somehow, as the Protestant church became westernized, we lost the understanding between the two ministries. I hope you find the information on ritual abuse informing and valuable as well. At the time of this writing, I work and operate in primarily, ritual abuse and exorcism ministry. But on occasion, I work with and equip deliverance ministers.

In your hands is M16 Ministries: *A Field Guide to Advanced Spiritual Warfare*, and I pray that the chapters that it contains will bless you and your ministry in the darker battles you may be facing. This guide is the result of M16 Ministries ten years in ministry, from counseling sessions, to deliverance, ritual abuse, and exorcism. You will find that this guide is essential in providing pastoral care to the afflicted soul.

-

CHAPTER 1

Introduction to Deliverance Ministry

When the seventy disciples returned from ministry (Luke 10), they were elated that the forces of darkness submitted to their spiritual authority. Jesus responded to them, "Behold, I have given you authority to tread on serpents and scorpions, and over all the power of the enemy, and nothing will injure you. Nevertheless do not rejoice in this, that the spirits are subject to you, but rejoice that your names are recorded in heaven" (Luke 10:19-20).

Jesus wanted the seventy disciples to rejoice in the fact that their souls were among the list of the eternally saved. Salvation is the single, most important point to walk away with, and it's the reason Jesus left us with the ministry of deliverance and the authority to tread on serpents—demonic spirits that are in our dominion. Demonic spirits hate God's creation called man. The forces of darkness know the best way to attack this spiritual being is to target his soul and make him ill. The primary objective of deliverance ministry is not to focus on the demonic, but rather to understand the spiritual warfare required to heal a soul that is spiritually sick.

Throughout Scripture, Jesus focused on bringing His love and compassion into the fallen human condition, breaking the curse of original

1

sin that we are all born into, and healing the congenitally sick heart and soul from this wretched curse through the Lord Jesus Christ. As Christians, it is imperative that we have a healthy, passionate heart and soul. Having a spiritually healthy heart and soul is critical to the first commandment Jesus gave us.

The Gospel of Matthew tells us why it is important to have a strong spirit and soul. The Scripture gives an account of an expert in the Mosaic Law who took it upon himself to challenge the knowledge and integrity of Jesus Christ. The expert in the Law thought he would put Jesus in His place with this question, "Teacher, which is the great commandment in the Law?" (Matthew 22:36). Jesus answered the expert in law by quoting from the book of Deuteronomy, "You shall love the Lord your God with all your heart and with all your soul and with all your might" (Deuteronomy 6:5). And Jesus added, "This is the great and foremost commandment" (Matthew 22:38).

We are to love our God with all our heart, soul, and strength. The greatest commandment is to go deeper in our relationship with Jesus. This deepening relationship is called a *transforming union*, where the soul learns to abandon its worldly ideology and become more like its indwelling, beloved Jesus Christ. When a soul meets the Savior, it can no longer live in the same sinful nature of this fallen world. It must change and align itself in spirit with the Holy Spirit.

For some believers, it may be difficult for them to love God with all their heart (spirit), and all their soul (minds), and all their strength (faith). Something dark and spiritual may be oppressing them, possibly a stronghold—a mind captive in thoughts contrary to the will of God, or a soul wound—where painful memories and emotions hinder the spiritual progress of this individual. In more severe cases, spiritual oppression, obsession, curses, or even possession could be the root issue in the soul's impeded spiritual advancement. A severely oppressed soul is *spiritually afflicted*. Affliction means the soul is in distress. There are both positive and negative connotations to a soul being afflicted. When a righteous person is biblically fasting, he is willfully inhibiting his soul from its soulish desire for food. Prayer and fasting is a positive spiritual form of afflicting the soul. When a demon afflicts the soul through oppression, this is, of course, negative.

The oppressed, afflicted soul, is spiritually ill and suffering from ungodly thoughts. The late Leanne Payne called these ungodly thoughts *diseased attitudes*.[1] The minister must allow the Holy Spirit to lead in discerning whether the root stronghold is demonic, or the root is ungodly thoughts from a soul wound or severe trauma from childhood. The current trend for deliverance ministries is only to focus on demonic strongholds. This approach is ineffective because it excludes the inner healing process for the heart and soul. The common approach is to deliver the afflicted soul from demons, and that's the end of ministry.

Tormented souls require much more than deliverance prayer ministry to receive a full inner healing. The soul still retains the pain and trauma memories that granted the demons access in the first place. The soul still has scars from the oppression. The soul must submit its inner healing to Jesus. Jesus is the one who brings inner healing to the soul. Jesus will walk the soul to its victory. A soul that can't move forward in its healing process is stuck. A soul that is stuck is in bondage to a lie of hopelessness. In this state, the soul is in jeopardy of becoming re-demonized and more deeply oppressed. The afflicted soul may feel completely helpless. But it's not. God promised, through His prophet Isaiah, "The Spirit of the Lord God is upon me, because the Lord has anointed me to bring good news to the afflicted; He has sent me to bind up the brokenhearted, to proclaim liberty to captives and freedom to prisoners" (Isaiah 61:1).

God promised of the coming of the Messiah, the Lord Jesus Christ. He would bring his ministry of healing wounded hearts and breaking the soul free from strongholds and bondage. God is prophetically referring to deliverance and inner healing ministry. It is through Jesus, not a minister, that healing comes to the soul. God sent His Son to minister in this capacity. Jesus fulfilled God's promise. In the Gospel of Luke, Scripture tells us, "The Spirit of the Lord is upon me, because He anointed me to

---

1 Leanne Payne, *Restoring the Christian Soul (Grand Rapids: Zondervan, 2006)*, 27.

preach the gospel to the poor, He has sent me to proclaim release to the captives, and recovery of site to the blind, to set free those who are oppressed" (Luke 4:18).

Jesus's ministry of deliverance is the freeing of a soul from spiritual affliction. Healing the soul also involves healing the spirit from any heart wounds that may have opened or festered from oppression or severe trauma. In these heart wounds are rooted ungodly beliefs and attitudes the soul believes about itself. Demonic attachments tend to be rooted in wounded hearts. It's common for ministries to separate the inner healing of the brokenhearted from the deliverance, which, when coupled together, brings liberty to the captive soul. Since these two ministries can't be separated, many times deliverance doesn't happen because the heart is spiritually wounded. Other times, deliverance will happen, but a full healing doesn't occur because a hidden heart wound surfaces as the root of the demonic affliction. Keep in mind, the inner healing and the deliverance are one ministry. Many ministries choose to avoid the inner healing portion because it may require a long-term commitment to an individual, so they don't consider healing the heart wound.

The miracle of the cross gives the body of Christ, you and me, the power and authority in this ministry to tread over the demonic ground forces of darkness on this earth. Jesus was victorious on the cross. He destroyed the works of Satan from having any eternal effects on us. We live in a biblical dispensation of time between the work of Jesus Christ defeating death on the cross and Jesus returning. During this time, the satanic angelic kingdom is defeated but not powerless. Even though the satanic angels are defeated, they still possess their free will.

The kingdom of darkness is waiting for its judgment. The satanic heavenly realm is infuriated about its defeat and is carrying out collateral damage against you and I. God allows this evil to happen on earth. We are living on a spiritual battlefield. During our lives we may encounter evil, we may allow it to seduce us, or we confront it through the righteousness of Jesus Christ. The reason we live on this earth in our mortal bodies is to choose Jesus Christ and His gift of eternal life. Those souls who don't choose Jesus Christ to be their lord and savior will remain in the Adamic fallen state of original sin forever. When the flesh dies in a state of fallen sin, the soul is doomed to perish in eternal separation from God. For this reason, the forces of darkness work overtime to prevent souls from choosing an eternity in paradise with the Lord Jesus Christ. This spiritual battle is what allows God to demonstrate his glory and power. The secondary reason you live this life in a body of flesh is the transformation of your soul so that you prepare yourself for an eternity with the Lord Jesus Christ. Our soul, embodied in flesh, must work to transform itself to be more Christ-like. It is the transformed soul that will spend eternity with Jesus in heaven.

Transformational Ministry from Glory to Glory

The purpose of deliverance ministry is to help those souls stuck in their spiritual advancement or souls that are spiritually afflicted. When our spiritual being is given the gift of eternal life through the Lord Jesus Christ, our soul must undergo some spiritual transformations.

> "Now the Lord is the Spirit, and where the Spirit of the Lord is, there is liberty. But we all, with unveiled face, beholding as in a mirror the glory of the Lord, are being transformed into the same image from glory to glory, just as from the Lord, the Spirit."
> —2 Corinthians 3:17-18

When a soul is afflicted, wounded, or cursed, it will require ministry that helps realign its focus on Jesus. I want to comment here that a soul can be spiritually afflicted and also be completely focused on Jesus. I have worked with people who are absolute saints yet have severe demonic attacks from spiritual doorways they didn't open. An example of such a person would be the Catholic mystic Padre Pio, who died in the late 1960s. Padre Pio was a miracle worker who was severely attacked by Satan. I know of other such saints who also experience this form of torment, but they are rare.

A severe affliction can also come from a cursed bloodline, such as a lineage of witchcraft, Freemasonry, or false Christian doctrines such as Mormonism and Jehovah Witnesses. Souls that are Christ-centric can also be cursed generationally through bloodlines. Just keep this in the back of your mind as you minister. Also, these people can go through transforming union with God even though a curse exists. I want to shut down the common church doctrine that just because a soul is afflicted, it is through a person's open door of sin. Many times, people are cursed because of their own sinful behavior. It's important to remember that each case is unique, and there is no methodology in working with these souls. You will encounter situations where only God has the answer, and He isn't sharing it with you. God is God, and He doesn't owe us answers. You will encounter cases where curse breaking doesn't work. As an example, I have seen severely cursed bloodlines from Freemasonry that may take years to break. Just because you have an ancestor in the Masons doesn't mean you're cursed. I am referring to the severe cases I have ministered with firsthand. These cases shows up from time to time. The curses don't break with methodical curse-breaking prayers. God won't always give revelation as to what is going on. God will assist you through supplication and prayer. He may give you revelation or He may not. That's just the way He works. When these situations arise, I direct ministers to Proverbs: "It is the glory of God to conceal a matter, but the glory of kings is to search out a matter" (Proverbs 25:2).

Each soul is a new unique creation of God. Therefore, each ministry session is also unique. The contemporary Christian doctrine on deliverance now is to pray, then bind this demon or that demon, and if it is a woman, bind the Jezebel spirit. I call this *methodology deliverance*. It's mainstream in ministry because it involves a process anybody can use. Every Christian book on deliverance contains this methodology. The popularity is widespread because of Christian publishing media. It sells books and DVDs. If you're involved in a deliverance ministry, you will need to abandon these cookie-cutter best-seller teachings. They're not suitable for spiritual warfare ministry. The reason this is ineffective is that it is a process, and demons have already figured this out.

Popular Deliverance Methodologies and Doctrines

These published prayer methodologies have become popular, and some churches and ministers have built deliverance schools around these doctrines. Most of the curriculum of these schools comes out of the contemporary classic deliverance books, such as *Pigs in the Parlor*, or *The Practical Guide to Deliverance* by Frank and Ida Mae Hammond, and *Bondage Breakers* by Neal Anderson. These books are instrumental in teaching deliverance, but the problem is they are very dated and behind the times. The Holy Spirit has been revealing more to us about this ministry. Holy Spirit-led ministry requires that we listen to Him. Process-based ministry can be executed without involving the Holy Spirit. In methodical curse breaking, even a New Age minister can cast out a demon in the name of Jesus. I have seen some deliverance ministers build up a library of prayers for every kind of curse possible. Be very careful about not being led down a road of deception. When you exclude the Holy Spirit in ministry, you are operating under your own pride. These early works were instrumental in raising up deliverance ministers. What I have seen occurring in ministry is that ministers are relying strictly on these curse-breaking prayers. It is not these prayers that set people free; it is Jesus Christ who liberates and heals the afflicted soul. In ministry, we must surrender to the will of the Father and follow the guidance of the Holy Spirit. It is paramount that the minister listen to the Holy Spirit and knows His voice.

Maturity is another factor in this ministry. There are times where a demon won't leave because of God's timing on the healing. The spiritually immature minister will not hear from God that it is a timing thing, and the minister will seek another deliverance prayer to break the affliction. I can dispute this process because I have already been down this road early on in my ministry. The Holy Spirit convicted me of this some time ago. Unfortunately, this methodology is still prevailing in the church and deliverance ministry today. As God heals the heart and the soul, we must listen to Him and follow what He's doing. We must also wait on his timing if the deliverance is not going as we planned. Some transformations and healings are instant, and many other times the healings are very long term. As the minister, you must remove your pride and bring the compassion of Jesus Christ into every prayer session. It's not about which prayer you're bringing for ministry, it's about who you're bringing to the prayer session: Jesus!

Holy Spirit-Driven Liberation Prayer Ministry

About a year ago, I was called out to a small church to pray for deliverance. The pastor told me that he and his wife did a lot of curse breaking with a young woman named Tonya. The pastor said over the phone that he had cast out all these spirits, using curse-breaking prayer methodology. Tonya was still experiencing oppression, even though he prayed to expel the spirit of Jezebel from her the night before. Tonya wasn't moving forward in her battle with whatever was oppressing her. I agreed to come over to the pastor's church and meet with Tonya.

At the meeting with Tonya, I sat down in the pastor's office and did the basic meet and greet. The pastor wanted to jump in, right away, and do some more binding and casting out of spirits. I requested that we hold off until I could hear from Tonya her story of what was happening to her and why she felt oppressed. Whenever I go to a deliverance prayer session, I am always the biggest skeptic, and I make the prayer recipient prove to me that what is going on is demonic. A majority of the ministers are far too eager to jump in with warfare prayer before understanding what is going on, so I do my interview session and I just let the person requesting ministry tell me his or her story.

For Tonya, she was returning home soon to the Ukraine and wanted to be set free of this oppression before leaving. She told me about her stronghold of anger she held toward her mother. She said she was angry at her mom for running her father out of her life when she was very young. Her mom did not allow Tonya or her siblings to contact him. From a counseling perspective, the first flag went up for parental attachment issues. The father is missing, and Tonya's angry toward Mom. There is a soul wound here that will take time to heal. I also took notes on all the negative comments she made about herself. These are ungodly beliefs she held and believed about herself. These are *diseased attitudes.*

This session illustrates why it's good just to let people share their story with you first. I let Tonya tell her story for well over an hour. Then she told me about how her little brother molested her when she was only six years old. I paused Tonya at this pivotal revelation. I asked her how old her little brother was, to verify if I'd heard that important piece of information correctly. Tonya said her brother was only four years old, and he would come into her bedroom at night and try to have sex with her. I paused Tonya again at this startling revelation. I asked Tonya if she would deem this as normal behavior for a little four-year-old boy? How did this little boy acquire this unnatural behavior? Tonya just stared back at me for a moment, puzzled. She didn't say anything for a moment and then I watched her eyes tear up. She finally responded, "Oh my god! My father was molesting my brother! That's why my mom threw him out and didn't want us contacting him. All these years I hated my mother, and she was protecting us!" Tonya just wept for some time as the Holy Spirit delivered her from decades of anger. The Holy Spirit took the ministry session down a path the process style session completely missed. This critical revelation through the Holy Spirit set Tonya free!

Issues with Process-Driven Prayer Deliverance Ministry

My primary concern with methodical process-driven prayer ministry is that it has a limited scope. *Bondage Breakers* and *Pigs in the Parlor* have their merits in bringing up untrained ministers into spiritual warfare. For new ministers seeking information on transgressions and generational curses, these books are a great place to start. This material is useful for the most basic cases that surface in the church. However, as I write this book, we are living in the times of 2 Timothy 3, where we see the rise of the occult. "Just as Jannes and Jambres opposed Moses, so these men also oppose the truth, men of depraved mind, rejected in regard to the faith. But they will not make further progress; for their folly will be obvious to all, just as Jannes's and Jambres's folly was also" (2 Timothy 3:8-9).

Jannes and Jambres were the sorcerers, the occultists, in Pharaoh's court, who could replicate most of the plagues sent by God. This verse in Timothy seems to resonate with what is happening today in our society.

The people I have been encountering in my spiritual warfare ministry battles are the Jannes and the Jambres. The occult is on the rise, and the current church can't fathom the depths of its pure evil. I'm finding occult activity has become prevalent as I minister with ritual abuse survivors and witness firsthand what the occult can do. The occult has used mind control and has programmed innocent children for rituals. This falls under the umbrella of Dissociative Identity Disorder (DID) prayer ministry. I have witnessed demons move in and out of ritual abuse survivors, as well as occultists astral project into people during ministry sessions. During these sessions, the curse-breaking prayers used by most deliverance ministers are out of the scope of usefulness in these situations. DID prayer ministry is altogether different from deliverance ministry. In fact, deliverance prayer can do more harm than any good to those who have fractured souls and are experiencing occult attacks. The methodical deliverance prayers don't cover too many aspects of the occult and how they do their evil things.

Spiritual warfare is never cut and dry. The best approach for this degree of warfare is to live a life that includes fasting. Listen to the Holy Spirit on what is going on during battle and walk in your spiritual authority. At this level of warfare, you will find yourself using the appropriate Scripture as the Holy Spirit gives you words of knowledge and wisdom. Classic and popular deliverance ministry prayers are all ineffective when it comes to occult battles. My intention here is not to knock the classic approach, but to expand upon it and equip you with the understanding of a much bigger picture. I envision spiritual warfare as three separate ministry components:

1. an office of deliverance ministry (bondage breaking and low-level demonic warfare),
2. an office of exorcism (high level demonic and angelic realms), and
3. an office of ritual abuse prayer ministry (restoring shattered lived and spiritual direction through inner healing).

Keep in mind, these offices are of great importance, and starting in one doesn't promote you to another. God is the one who fills these offices with His ministers. God is the one who fights these battles. The successful people I have met across denominations, Protestant and Catholic, were not called to these positions of office; they were drafted into battle by God!

Pastoral Care for the Soul

Jesus's ministry of deliverance is about healing demonic afflictions of the human soul. As a deliverance minister, we may be required to discern if the prayer recipient is stuck in his path, whether it's through clarifying his salvation or helping in the sanctification of the soul. Be aware there is more to deliverance ministry than this. Understanding an individual's spiritual walk and development of his soul in the transforming union is critical and revealing for ministry direction. There is no process or steps to take in deliverance ministry. The deliverance minister must be following the will of the Father. It is Jesus and Jesus alone who brings the deliverance and healing. We are merely coparticipants, through prayer and standing in our spiritual authority. The deliverance minister's job is not to focus on battling demons but to aid in realigning the afflicted soul and spirit to Jesus. We minister to the afflicted soul using three primary types of ministry:

1. low-level demonic deliverance (demonic oppression).
2. through liberation prayers for the exorcism of high order demons and satanic angels (occult and possession).
3. through prayer ministry for survivors of severe trauma (dissociative identity disorder and ritual abuse).

Our job is to make the soul focus or refocus back on Jesus! We don't fight their battles; the afflicted souls must do that out of their own free will with Jesus.

CHAPTER 2

Sin and the Soul

What is God's purpose of sin? There are a lot of misconceptions and false doctrines in the church revolving around this critical topic of sin. The biggest misleading issue we have of sin is its association with the human soul and eternal damnation. We have all heard the fire and brimstone sermons of sinners going to hell. Worse yet, there are Christian evangelists on street corners calling out people and their sins, telling them they are sinners and they are going to hell. Is sin a metric that determines whether or not we go to hell, or biblically, is it something else? "For all have sinned and fall short of the glory of God" (Romans 3:23).

According to the apostle Paul, in his epistle to the Romans, all of us have sinned and fallen short of God's desires for us. From this perspective, being a sinner also includes the street evangelist with the bullhorn shouting out everyone's sins. The apostle Paul tells us that sin seems to be a metric with God on how we have fallen short with him. God uses sin to help the soul identify where it needs improvement. The purpose of sin is not for inflicting God's judgment on the soul.

> "The Lord is not slow about his promise, as some count slowness, but is patient toward you, not wishing for any to perish but for all to come to repentance."
> —2 Peter 3:9

13

God wants your soul to repent from sin. Repent means that your heart feels remorse for its sinful actions. The epistle of the apostle Peter reveals that God doesn't want your soul to perish. This piece of information paints a different picture from the fire and brimstone sermon. We are all God's creation, and His desire is that not one soul perish in eternal damnation. Eternal salvation has nothing to do with how good or bad you are. God's plan for salvation is rather simple. It's a decision. Repent from your sinful life and ask the Lord Jesus Christ for His forgiveness. As your heart and soul go to Jesus, He helps you and shows you how to live a more righteous life. When a heart repents, it changes. The soul receives salvation through the grace and mercy of God.

For God So Loved the World

To properly understand sin, we must understand, to the best of our abilities, who God is and why God created us in the first place. Scripture reveals that God created us to demonstrate His love for us. It was His plan from the beginning for us to co-participate and co-rule with Him in his creation. Not only would we rule, but we would be in His presence "just as He chose us in Him before the foundation of the world, that we would be holy and blameless before Him in love" (Ephesians 1:4).

We know from Scripture that God bankrupted heaven and He sacrificed His son for the only true atonement of our sins. "For God so loved the world, that He gave His only begotten Son, that whoever believes in Him shall not perish, but have eternal life" (John 3:16). God's nature is love. Even though mankind was, and still is, in complete rebellion to Him, even from our very beginning in the garden of Eden, God loves us. Because God loves us, He sent his son, Jesus Christ, to take the full brunt of His wrath and judgment in our place. Jesus went to the cross in love and obedience to His Father in heaven.

> *"But so that the world may know that I love the Father, I do exactly as the Father commanded Me. Get up, let us go from here."*
> —*John 14:31*

At the cross, God demonstrated His love for us and His desire for reconciliation. In our rebellious, original sinful state, we can't live eternally in heaven with God, but it is God's desire for us to spend eternity with Him in heaven. All of God's interactions with us through prayer, deliverance, inner healing, and healing miracles, are demonstrations of His absolute love for us. The only thing God desires from us is our love toward Him and reconciliation. Through love and reconciliation, we receive the Son, Jesus Christ, as our lord and savior. Through Jesus, we receive the gift of eternal life.

God Created Man in His Image

In God's account of creation, He created two kinds of spiritual beings: angelic creatures and man. God created the angelic beings first. Why were the angels created? First, and foremost, God is a mystery. We don't know why God does things or what moves Him. From what He reveals in His Word, we can tell that God apparently wanted to create an everlasting supernatural heavenly kingdom. It has a hierarchy with a government, and even commerce. Angels hold offices and positions in heaven. Some angels guard the throne of God, and other angels do marvelous things in God's spiritual realm. There are even rulers and powers in God's kingdom, and what exactly they do is not clear to us. What is clear in the revelation we receive about heaven, through Scripture, is that God wants His spiritual creations to work with Him. He wants his creatures to participate with Him in carrying out His eternal plans.

God created all His spiritual beings with free will. We are not mindless slaves to Him. God's highest ranking angel, Lucifer, started an angelic rebellion in heaven because he wanted to be God. The angel Lucifer sinned through pride, greed, envy, the pursuit of power, and rebellion. When the rebellion failed, Lucifer and one-third of the angels—the ones that followed him and sinned, including rulers, princes, and armies (demons)—were expelled from heaven.

Two-thirds of God's angels remained loyal to Him in His heavenly realm. God is never alone; His angels surround Him. Even if the angels didn't exist, He is a triune God—Father, Son, and Holy Spirit. The spiritual being called man certainly wasn't needed by God, so why was it necessary to create us?

> "When I consider Your heavens, the work of Your fingers, the moon and the stars, which You have ordained; what is man that You take thought of him, and the son of man that You care for him?"
> —Psalm 8:3-4

God's primary attribute is love.[1] God wants to demonstrate His absolute love. Somewhere in this cosmic mystery, God decided to create a physical universe inside His spiritual realm and create mankind. These new spiritual beings, man, differed from His angelic spiritual creatures, in that man would have a physical embodiment of flesh. With this new creation God chose, by design, to interact and commune with us and, most of all, love us. Furthermore, God created us to co-participate with Him in his creation. For this to happen, we had to somehow share some spiritual DNA with the Creator and resemble Him in some way.

> "Then God said, 'Let Us make man in Our image, according to Our likeness; and let them rule over the fish of the sea and over the birds of the sky and over the cattle and over all the earth, and over every creeping thing that creeps on the earth.' God created man in his own image, in the image of God He created him; male and female He created them."
> —Genesis 1:26-27

The Father, the Son, and the Holy Spirit, are the superior Trinity. God created man as a spiritual being. He created us as a lesser, inferior image of the Trinity with soul and spirit embodied in flesh. In the garden, God communed with the inferior trinity, man. There was no evil found in the man, Adam. He had not eaten from the Tree of Knowledge of Good and Evil. Man's soul was God-centric. God created man's soul to be spiritually aligned and in tune with the Holy Spirit. Being spiritually aligned means that the soul is willfully surrendering to the will of the Holy Spirit and doesn't have desires of the flesh. In the garden, man's spirit operated in union with God's Spirit. God created man in His image to have a loving

---

1 1 John 4:8

relationship with him. We were created as spiritual beings to interact with God. The man was created in His image to model himself after Jesus Christ. We are to imitate Jesus and become more like Him. The only way to imitate Jesus is to know Jesus. We build friendships with other people by developing a deeper relationship with them. The relationship was Jesus's plan for us when he created the man and the woman.

Dominion and Obedience

God's plan for man was to be partner, and co-rule in his creation. God placed His creation, the man, and the woman into his mystical garden. Before man's fall into sin, the man and the woman had it pretty good in the garden of Eden. God manifested the garden and all the man and the woman had to do was cultivate it.[2] Man, which we know God named Adam, was given dominion over the earth.[3] The woman was later named Eve, after the fall in the garden. Dominion is a legal title; it has an authority and a governing aspect to it. This title was given both to the man, Adam, and the woman. Through the bloodline of Adam's rib, Eve received the title of headship. Adam and the woman held the keys to the earth. They were the legally governing body over all the earth under the authority of their creator, the Lord Jesus Christ. This dominion and legality over the earth is a major theme that starts in Genesis 1 and soon comes under dispute in Genesis 3. This conflict over sovereignty continues through the Bible and mankind's history, when Jesus confronted the issue in the desert with the temptation of Satan[4], and later defeated Satan at the cross.

The requirements God outlines in His ruling partnership with mankind is that we choose to obey Him. In the midst of the garden of Eden were two supernatural trees, the Tree of Life and the Tree of Knowledge of Good and Evil. Scripture only seems to identify one specific command for man to obey, and that was to not eat from the Tree of Knowledge of Good and Evil.

---

2 Genesis 2:15
3 Genesis 1:26
4 Luke 4

"The Lord God commanded the man, saying, 'From any tree of the garden you may eat freely; but from the tree of the knowledge of good and evil you shall not eat, for in the day that you eat from it you will surely die.'"
—*Genesis 2:16-17*

I believe God had to provide man with a means to demonstrate acts of obedience and submission to God's authority. Remember, the Mosaic Law was not in existence yet. God wanted a relationship with us. All relationships have boundaries that define, strengthen, or destroy them. Through obedience, we build a healthy relationship with God. Boundaries also demonstrate maturity and willingness to co-participate with another person. Our free will must surrender to the grace, authority, and love of the one true God.

The Original Sin

The biblical sense of sin is when the soul freely commits an act of disobedience against the will of God. You're probably aware of the adage, "The devil made me do it!" The devil doesn't make us sin. He may encourage the temptation for us to sin. For every wrongdoing in your life, your soul is responsible for making these bad decisions. Have you ever realized, too, that the natural desire for your soul is to be sinful rather than righteous? The reason we struggle in our sanctification and being righteous is because of the original sin. Original sin is inherited sin, which has affected all mankind since the fall of Adam and Eve in the garden of Eden.

The original sin began when Satan deceived the woman in the garden of Eden. Once again, this is a mystical garden; it has one foot in the spirit realm and another in our physical reality. God and his angels walked through this garden with Adam and the woman. There are also, apparently, animals in this garden. We can only speculate what God's nursery for the planet earth may have looked like at the dawn of creation. The garden was a supernatural heaven-like manifestation on earth.

The recount of the fall of man in the book of Genesis tells of a serpent in the Tree of Knowledge of Good and Evil speaking to the woman, Eve. I believe the serpent to be the fallen angel, now titled Satan, because in the apostle John's book of Revelation, Satan is called the dragon, a serpent (Revelation 12:9). The behavior of the serpent and his contradicting of the Word of God is also a clear indicator that this was Satan. Look how Satan twisted God's commands when he spoke to Eve: "Now the serpent was more crafty than any beast of the field which the Lord God had made. And he said to the woman, 'Indeed, has God said, "You shall not eat from any tree of the garden"?'" (Genesis 3:1).

Eve at this point was blameless and innocent, free of any sin. She was caught off guard by the serpent's comments. She may have been unaware of lies or what they were. So Eve stopped to address the serpent and what he said to her. "The woman said to the serpent, 'From the fruit of the trees of the garden we may eat; but from the fruit of the tree which is in the middle of the garden, God has said, "You shall not eat from it or touch it, or you will die"'" (Genesis 3:2-3).

Satan again responded by twisting the words God said: "The serpent said to the woman, 'You surely will not die! For God knows that in the day you eat from it your eyes will be opened, and you will be like God, knowing good and evil'" (Genesis 3:4). The deceiving words of Satan penetrated Eve's consciousness. The fiery darts of temptation now burned through her mind. What was this secret knowledge that God had deliberately held back from her? Eve gave into her desire to acquire this ungodly knowledge. Where have we seen this played out before? The anointed cherub Lucifer wanted to be like God.[5] Satan stoked the desires of the woman to seek the ungodly knowledge. Eve lusted for the secret knowledge.

"When the woman saw that the tree was good for food, and that it was a delight to the eyes, and that the tree was desirable to make one wise, she took from its fruit and ate; and she gave also to her husband with her, and he ate" (Genesis 3:6). Eve allowed herself to be deceived by Satan. She fell into committing a transgression against God. "For it was Adam who was first created, and then Eve. And it was not Adam who was deceived, but the woman being deceived, fell into transgression" (1 Timothy 2:13-14).

---

5 Isaiah 14:13-14

Eve acted on her temptation of the flesh and desired to eat the food from the forbidden tree. She lusted with her eyes and saw that the fruit was beautiful. "For all that is in the world, the lust of the flesh and the lust of the eyes and the boastful pride of life, is not from the Father, but is from the world" (1 John 2:16).

Eve gave into the sin of pride, just like Satan did, to become godlike. And her husband, who was commanded directly by God not to eat from this tree, also ate from it. This disobedience toward God is the nature of original sin. We allow thoughts and lusts of the flesh and self-pride to enter our minds. It was in this manner that Adam and Eve allowed themselves to fall to their sinful nature. Their downfall was disobedience and rebellion to God's simple command.

Adam and Eve possessed God-given titles of being rulers over all creation. When they disobeyed God, they subjugated themselves and all mankind over to Satan. Adam and Eve had a high-level ruling governmental position. It was their spiritual title they handed over to Satan as they became slaves to him. Through their surrendered headship, Satan acquired all the kingdoms of the earth, which he used to tempt Jesus with (Luke 4). Satan didn't truly have the kingdoms, he only presumed to have them under the legalistic titles of Adam and the woman. How did this happen? Jesus told us we can't serve two masters.[6] We either serve God or we serve the flesh (Satan). When you rebel against God, you serve Satan.

Not only was the entire human race now subjugated to Satan's dominion, but we all experienced an interior spiritual realignment. The soul's spiritual alignment was inverted. No longer was the soul focused on the spirit and Christ-centric, as it was prior in the garden. With the disobedience and giving into temptations of lust and pride, the soul now focused on the flesh and not the spirit. The human spirit at the moment of original sin became unrighteous and could no longer be in the presence of God. A human spirit that is separate from God is spiritually dead.

"Therefore, just as through one man sin entered into the world,

---

6 Matthew 6:24

*and death through sin, and so death spread to all men, because
all sinned."*
—Romans 5:12

Through disobedience, mankind experienced both physical and spiritual death. The entire bloodline of the human race, through the ruling titles of the man and woman, was enslaved in the curse. The original sin was an inherited sin to all mankind. At that moment in the garden, we were all cursed to become slaves to mankind's new master, Satan. Man must be purchased back from his slave master. God loved us even though we disobeyed Him in the garden. God promised us that He would redeem us. Redemption is an old phrase used in the slave trade, meaning to purchase. God redeemed us at the cross through the price of the ultimate sacrifice of the blood of his Son, Jesus Christ. God made the first promise of sending his Son to undo what Satan did in the garden.

"And I will put enmity between you and the woman, and between your seed and her seed; he shall bruise you on the head, and you shall bruise him on the heel."
—Genesis 3:15

God prophetically revealed His plan to send a redeemer through a virgin birth. When God spoke of seed, He was speaking of the reproductive DNA from a male. The woman's reproductive part is her womb and does not have seed. This proclamation was God's promise of Jesus Christ coming to redeem us through a virgin birth. God told Satan that His Son would bruise Satan's head. The head represents Satan's power and authority. God foretold the work on the cross, where Satan would bruise Jesus Christ on the heel. The promise from God at this incident is that His Son, Jesus Christ, would defeat the work and powers of Satan on the cross. And as we all know, God's promise was true and fulfilled over two thousand years ago at Calvary.

"And Jesus came up and spoke to them, saying, 'All authority has been given to Me in heaven and on earth'."
—Matthew 28:18

The work of Jesus Christ starts in Genesis and continues through to the book of Revelation. Every baby ever born is born with the soul inverted to the desires of the flesh and the spirit born dead. Even though God redeemed us through his Son, Jesus Christ, mankind is still born under this spiritually inherited curse. When the soul chooses Jesus Christ, the soul is flipped back into alignment with the indwelling Jesus and the human spirit is quickened to life.

Imputed Sin

We experience original sin as an inherited sin. We are all born into this world as sinners with our soul naturally inclined to sin. Our natural soulish behavior is to rebel against God. Our sinful nature enslaves us to Satan. The consequence of sin is death. It is this inherited sin that causes our bodies to decay and die. From Adam to Moses, the sin of man primarily fell under inherited sin. The ultimate penalty for their sinful nature was death..Then when God had Moses introduce the Law to His people, the consequences of sin were now twofold: inherited sin from the original sin, and now *imputed sin* from breaking the Law. Imputed sin means to transfer sin from one man to another. Under the Law, sins that were committed against the Law were imputed specifically to the sinner. When Moses introduced the Law, the wages of sin were death, both from the inherited original sinful nature and now for the transgressions against the laws of God, which is imputed sin. Why did God introduce this and why were the consequences of sin now twofold? God now used the Law and its concept of imputed sin to transfer sin from one man to another to bring about our salvation and redemption.

> *"Therefore, just as through one man sin entered into the world, and death through sin, and so death spread to all men, because all sinned—for until the Law sin was in the world, but sin is not imputed when there is no law. Nevertheless, death reigned from Adam until Moses, even over those who had not sinned in the likeness of the offense of Adam, who is a type of Him who was to come."*
> —Romans 5:12-14

When Jesus drank from the cup His Father prepared for Him, Jesus had led a sinless holy life. He was not conceived by man so He was not under the curse of inherited sin. The only way for Jesus to be born void of the curse of the original sin would be supernatural conception through the Holy Spirit. God also had to select a righteous woman, young Mary, to be His mother. Jesus was not born a sinner, nor did He ever commit an act of sin. The sin of the world was imputed to Jesus at the cross. On the cross, the Father in heaven treated Jesus as if He were guilty of all the sins ever committed—from the garden with Adam to the very last man who will ever walk the earth. Jesus took our sins upon Himself so we can be presented righteous before the heavenly Father. Jesus's atonement alone is the only way to eternal life with the heavenly Father.

The heavenly Father imputed our sin to Jesus, who was righteous. We receive the grace of this redeeming miracle simply by accepting Jesus Christ as our lord and savior.

> *"Therefore, we are ambassadors for Christ, as though God were making an appeal through us; we beg you on behalf of Christ, be reconciled to God. He made Him who knew no sin to be sin on our behalf, so that we might become the righteousness of God in Him."*
> —*2 Corinthians 5:20-21*

Temptation and Our Sin

The third form of sin is our personal sin. It is our freewill sin that afflicts our soul and opens toeholds and doorways to the enemy. Under personal sin, the soul needs to repent for its sinful behavior (addiction, anger, pornography, sexual perversion, alcoholism, emotional outbursts, and any other desires of the flesh). Repentance means a change of heart and that we feel remorse for our sinful actions. There are times the heart doesn't change immediately but makes very slight adjustments towards repentance. When God is working on your heart and soul, it may take some time to work things out. This soul changing process is called *sanctification*. God transforms the soul from glory to glory, and many times this walk can be very uncomfortable, emotional, and long in duration. A soul that is going through corrective tribulations needs spiritual direction and not deliverance. There are people who come to me wanting deliverance from their pornography addiction. They want a magic prayer to set them free, and they don't want to take responsibility for their soulish desires. Pornography addiction and sexual perversion are sanctification issues, not deliverance issues. If a demon is present and tormenting the soul with this behavior, then this is a different story. Whenever a Christian comes to me seeking deliverance, I make them prove to me they have a demonic affliction. Many times, they can't, and the deliverance minister must be the bearer of the bad news. These souls need spiritual direction and possibly even counseling; but their soul and heart must enter into repentance, by asking the Lord for forgiveness, and then start the long journey of having Jesus walk them out of their addiction.

Because of original sin, our soul has the natural desire to commit sin rather than obey God. The root origin of any sin we commit begins as a thought in our soul. Temptation is a desire to do evil that begins inside us. The devil doesn't make us do anything. Temptation is the inner urge, a spark to do evil, and then it stokes the sparks that become embers of lust. Lust, although typically sexual in nature, is an emotion that must be acted upon to become sin. Lust is the physical manifestation of sin in the soul. When we act upon desires of lust for power, sex, revenge, or addiction, to name a few, we commit sin.

> "But each one is tempted when he is carried away and enticed
> by his own lust. Then when lust has conceived, it gives birth to
> sin; and when sin is accomplished, it brings forth death."
> —James 1:14-15

A soul in union with God desires to not sin, but with the nature of original sin, thoughts of temptation are inevitable. Original sin is the internal spiritual conflict within ourselves as we battle temptation and lust. When the soul caves to lust, we commit sin, a transgression. Overwhelming thoughts of guilt result from the actions of the soul committing transgressions. Shame is an illness that overcomes the soul and wills itself to separate from God to hide from Him. The soul will hide itself from the indwelling Jesus in much the same way Adam hid his nakedness from God in the garden. The soul briefly loses its alignment from the spiritual and focuses back to the flesh. Only through repentance of the heart and prayer do we realign the soul back to being spiritual and Christ-centric. As God allows our soul to repent for sin, we must never take for granted the divine gift of grace and mercy.

Ministering to the Soul

I can write volumes on sin and its effects on the soul. Whenever people come to you for deliverance ministry, take the time to understand what is going on in their soul. Never start prayer ministry right away. Many times, people have cursed themselves for being unrepentant. They are stuck and they believe it's because either God has cursed them or God is putting them through a tribulation. Many souls just won't take responsibility for their actions and therefore get spiritually stuck. I have worked with far too many souls who worked with deliverance ministers who did nothing more than curse-breaking prayers with them. Curse breaking doesn't free a soul that is unrepentant in its sinful behavior. Souls focused on the flesh are out of spiritual alignment with the Holy Spirit. I have seen too many people give the devil too much credit for their own behaviors. They were doing the work for the demons. The first step in deliverance is understanding where the soul focuses on the flesh. What is out of spiritual alignment that is allowing or causing the demonic affliction of the soul? Is there even a demon present? How do you gain an understanding of what is going on with the soul? Here's a simple prayer I use all the time in ministry for this situation,

> *Jesus, could you please give us revelation on what is going on here?*

It's called *listening prayer*. I explain to the people I am working with that I don't expect an answer from them. I put that out there so Jesus can lead us down the right path in this individual soul's healing ministry. In the middle or latter part of the ministry session, you may see the answer unfold in front of you. The Holy Spirit is excellent about bringing direction in these sessions. One thing you'll also notice is there is no process or methodology in this book. The triune God heals; we just invite Him into the session and let Him do all the work. Start learning to rely on prayer and Jesus, because that's how miraculous healing manifests!

CHAPTER 3

Spiritual Alignment, Salvation, and the Soul

The Law of God can't make a person righteous. Through the Law of God comes the knowledge of sin. It is through the Law that our souls understand the guilt of our actions. The Law constrains the soul, which is capable of doing evil, to do what is right.

"For all who have sinned without the Law will also perish without the Law, and all who have sinned under the Law will be judged by the Law."
—Romans 2:12

Just obeying the Law methodically will not save your soul. It is the soul that takes the Law to heart in faith that it will be justified.[1] The apostle Paul said that the Law is spiritual; we follow the Law in faith and through our belief in God.[2] God provided man with the Law because we are capable of unspeakable evil. Although God can't stand sin, He uses our fallen state to demonstrate his glory and His love for us. The deeper the sin, the greater God's grace abounds even more.[3]

"So that, as sin reigned in death, even so grace would reign through righteousness to eternal life through Jesus Christ our

---

1 Romans 2:13
2 Romans 7:14
3 Romans 5:20

Lord."
—Romans 5:21

The Father in heaven sent His son, Jesus Christ, as an act of immeasurable love, to be the ultimate blood sacrifice and only atonement for our sins. It was Jesus alone who took the wrath of God for our sins, and only through Him are we raised from death.

Just as Adam acted as a legal authority and handed over our dominion to Satan, Jesus Christ acted in His title and authority as the King of Kings and restored our dominion. Jesus loved us while we were in our ungodly state. God calls out to us in our fallen state to come to Him and fall in love with Him.

Justification

When your soul truly accepts Jesus Christ as your savior, your heart repents. That means there is a change in your heart to abandon your pre-saved ungodly ways. Your soul has chosen to change from its focus on itself and to focus now on Jesus. At this moment, the soul receives the gift of eternal salvation. The soul is now forever united with Jesus. During the fall of man, the spiritual alignment inverted, placing the focus on the flesh instead of Jesus. The conversion of the soul is immediate; the soul's spiritual alignment is restored to focus on Jesus Christ. During this realignment, your spiritual being becomes righteous in the eyes of God through the miracle of grace and mercy.

> *"For by grace you have been saved through faith; and that not of*
> *yourselves, it is the gift of God."*
> *—Ephesians 2:8*

The resurrection of the soul from its fallen state is called *justification*. Justification is the act of being made righteous before God. The justification is a legal, spiritual process that has a bearing on whether the soul and spirit are given eternal life in heaven or eternal separation (damnation). A justified soul is a saved soul and spirit.

> *"Therefore, since we have been justified through faith, we have*
> *peace with God through our Lord Jesus Christ."*

—*Romans 5:1*

Under the curse of original sin, the human spirit is dead. Spiritual death is the separation of man's consciousness and his spirit from the presence of God.[4] When the soul is justified, the human spirit is no longer in a state of separation from God. The Holy Spirit quickens the human spirit to life.

> *"So also it is written, 'The first man, Adam, became a living*
> *soul.' The last Adam became a life-giving spirit."*
> —*1 Corinthians 15:45*

Jesus is the last Adam. Jesus came to complete what our common ancestor, the first Adam, failed to do. Jesus, under his supreme headship, restored the dominion squandered under Adam's headship. To restore our dominion, God had to reconcile with mankind. God the Father had to demonstrate His unconditional love for us by sending Jesus to become incarnate and be sacrificed for our sins. Jesus became the last Adam and lived a sinless, holy life during the three decades He lived on this earth. Jesus as a man had to demonstrate obedience to His heavenly Father. Jesus fulfilled his Father's will and drank from the Father's cup when He became our atonement on the cross.

> *"Anyone who is hung [on a cross] is cursed in the sight of God."*
> —*Deuteronomy 21:23.*

Jesus became the curse on the cross.

In deliverance ministry, you will encounter people whose salvations are questionable. A problem I have seen as a street minister is that too many pastors think if they get several people to accept Jesus on out-reaches in the streets, then they added more souls to the kingdom. Winning souls is an independent relational process, not a metric. Salvation requires a bit more than having the person at the coffee shop recite the sinner's prayer. It may make you feel good, but many times the salvation was incomplete. As a street minister, and after working in pagan festivals covertly, I learned firsthand that leading a soul to salvation could take a

---

4 Ephesians 2:1-5; Colossians 2:13

bit more time than we want to believe. It took several years with people before they turned their hearts to Him. There were lots of nudges and some deliverances along the way.

Jesus is wooing all His kids. In San Francisco, where I ministered on the streets, we saw supernatural signs and wonders. I saw broken bones miraculously healed through prayer. And maybe only 50 percent of these people who experienced definitive supernatural miracles were swayed to accept Jesus after seeing His signs and wonders. My team prayed for healing for a Satanist in the Haight-Ashbury district of San Francisco, and a five-hour-old broken ankle was healed through prayer. She got up and walked on it. She thanked us for praying for her healing but was unmoved to accept Jesus Christ as her lord and savior. What I learned on the streets is that you must understand where people are at in their spiritual walk and fall in step with what the Holy Spirit is doing there. We still pray for healing over all the souls who let us. But the miraculous sometimes is not enough for hardened hearts.

In ministry sessions, I have worked with people who lived cursed lives. The souls recited the sinner's prayer, but they never repented of their sin. Salvation requires action on the heart and soul's part. The soul must turn away from original sin and transform. Repentance requires a transformation of both the heart and soul.

For a soul to be justified, it needs more than a prayer; the heart must be repentant. Jesus told Pilate that to be saved he had to be reborn. A repentant heart is a reborn soul. For the unsaved and unrepentant soul there is more torment, and the soul doesn't understand why it is not receiving Jesus. The result is that the soul is frustrated and wondering why his life is such a mess.

I have even had overzealous Christians deliberately bring me unsaved children or relatives without telling them that they're taking them to a deliverance prayer session. This heartless action aggravates me. I don't like surprises like this dropped on me. It is controlling, manipulative, and sidesteps God's honoring of the soul's free will. Charismatic people tend to do this thinking if I cast out his demons, the person will accept Jesus. This spiritual reasoning is operating out of their pride and bypassing the work of the Holy Spirit on the unsaved individual. It's disrespectful to both the prayer minister and the person receiving prayer. In the zealous Christians' crazy scheming, and in their desperation, they believed a deliverance prayer session would magically save their loved one. I don't do deliverance prayer with the unsaved unless Jesus tells me to minister to an unsaved soul. There are some occasions where He will release you into ministering.

As an example, I occasionally minister at Burning Man, a pagan festival attended by over seventy thousand people, in the Nevada desert every year. One year I was ministering with a Reiki healer and her demon manifested. I was going to stop ministering with her when I heard the Holy Spirit tell me to cast the demon out. As I ministered with this woman, I found out she was raised Jewish. She knew the spirit was a demon. She allowed me to call on God's name of Elohim. I did as the Holy Spirit instructed me. The woman knew she was set free through that supernatural experience and abandoned Reiki healing altogether. The event was so life changing that she spent nine months tracking me down. Her therapist concluded she had a major paranormal experience and breakthrough. Off and on now, I get a phone call from my Burning Man friend who needs spiritual direction. She returned to her roots of Jewish heritage. The compass is getting closer to pointing to Jesus. A year ago I worked with her in casting out more demons that were generational. She wouldn't permit me to use the New Testament, so I used Scripture from the book of Isaiah that are prophecies and promises of the coming of Jesus. The demons didn't appreciate those Scriptures at all and were expelled by them. After a powerful session, she asked me what Scriptures I used, and I gave them to her. Slowly the lightbulb gets brighter. You must be patient.

My common approach is to just have a conversation with people about their spirituality and build their trust. By respecting their choices, as God does, I then get released by the people to pray for them. By doing this, I have planted the seed, and it allows an opportunity to demonstrate God's signs and wonders and build up people for a Jesus encounter. Then I back off and allow the Holy Spirit to do his work. When you meet anyone unsaved, bring Jesus's compassion into the situation. Give the pre-believers spiritual direction that can lead them to repent, and work with them on their salvation. Never get ahead of them on their journey of salvation. Justification is the most powerful healing in the Bible we can experience. It raises the dead and quickens the spirit.

Sanctification

Through the gift of justification, your spiritual being was made righteous in the eyes of God. Your soul is still operating in its natural state of original sin. The soul's free will must surrender to God's will and learn to behave righteously. The soul is stubborn and self-focused. It will go through some trials before it understands it can do nothing on its own. For through Christ, the soul can do all things, and on its own, it can't accomplish anything. Through sanctification, the soul must stay in its realignment of being focused on the Holy Spirit.

> "Such were some of you; but you were washed, but you were sanctified, but you were justified in the name of the Lord Jesus Christ and by the Spirit of our God."
> —1 Corinthians 6:11

Sanctification is your lifelong battle of the flesh (sin) and your spirit's will to follow the conviction of the Holy Spirit. Sanctification requires fighting against sin, tearing down strongholds, and fighting off the attacks of the enemy. Sanctification is the transformation of the soul as it makes choices to eat from the Tree of Life rather than from the Tree of Knowledge of Good and Evil.

> "Now may the God of peace Himself sanctify you entirely; and may your spirit and soul and body be preserved complete, without blame at the coming of our Lord Jesus Christ"
> (1 Thessalonians 5:23).

Sanctification is the lifelong journey of your soul as it learns to become more Christ-like. On this journey, the indwelling Holy Spirit speaks to your soul and walks you out of your sinful nature and mindsets. Your soul will endure many trials and tribulations. Some of these trials can be so intense that many believers may misinterpret them as curses. The primary reason for these trials and tribulations are to transform the soul away from its sinful mindsets. Transformation comes from hearing God internally and through his Word. In a transforming union, the soul strives to imitate the indwelling Jesus.

> *"But we all, with unveiled face, beholding as in a mirror the glory of the Lord, are being transformed into the same image from glory to glory, just as from the Lord, the Spirit"*
> —*2 Corinthians 3:18*

Spiritually mature souls will despise lengthy tribulations but find inner joy in the rest of the presence of the indwelling Jesus. To summarize, this is a love-hate relationship. The soul hates the tribulation but loves the presence of the indwelling Jesus. The mature soul knows it is Jesus who will deliver it from the tribulation. Spiritual maturity is your soul developing a supernatural mindset that God will always deliver you through these trials. A spiritually mature soul submits more quickly to the will of the Father.

> *"Because the mind set on the flesh is hostile toward God; for it does not subject itself to the law of God, for it is not even able to do so."*
> —*Romans 8:7*

An immature soul with little spiritual development will not focus on its sanctification. This soul will misinterpret God's trials and tribulations as curses. The immature soul will ignore or not recognize the gentle urges of the Holy Spirit speaking from within.

I receive a lot of requests for deliverance from people who are dealing with pornography and sexual perversion. Men will ask me for deliverance ministry, but I tell them they need counseling. These men rarely elect to sit through counseling. They push for deliverance ministry, which they believe will be a magic prayer bullet healing for them. Sexual and pornography addiction are the most brutal addictions to be set free from, and it affects the person on multiple levels of his heart and soul. Sexual addiction is a nontrivial sanctification issue that requires walking the soul out of its bondage.

The addiction brings in diseased attitudes and corrupts the imagination, will, and the intellect of the soul. Guilt and shame are not the only things that sneak in with sexual addiction. Self-hatred always slips in as a diseased attitude.

One gentleman I worked with, Tim, was addicted to sex. Tim would go to Asian massage parlors in San Francisco after work and solicit the prostitutes there. I told Tim that the young women he was soliciting were indentured slaves from Asia. The addiction twists the intellect into ungodly (Tree of Knowledge of Good and Evil) reasoning. This individual was living under the deception that the women he was paying to have sex with were not trafficked slaves. This ungodly reasoning was dumbfounding to me how the Christian intellect can allow itself to be so deceived that it can't see the truth.

Tim refused to believe that the reality of his addiction involved sex slaves. Tim told me he quoted Scripture every time the urge came to him to solicit prostitutes. I reminded Tim that even Satan used Scripture (see Luke 4). Tim needed to go deeper and listen to the convictions of the Holy Spirit. I told Tim he needed to manifest the presence of Jesus Christ with him next time he went to solicit prostitutes. If Tim would practice this mental prayer exercise, he probably wouldn't take Jesus into the massage brothel. Tim looked at me and told me that I was completely New Age and walked out of the counseling session. He never returned. Tim had diseased attitudes about himself. He believed the lie of Satan that he could never be free of his addiction to sex. The demonic lie was that Tim believed he would receive instant deliverance from his original sinful nature of lusting for flesh. The lies in his soul told him that the indwelling Jesus wasn't sufficient to walk him out of his sex addiction.

Too many of Tim's church friends pointed him to deliverance ministry when what Tim needed was spiritual direction on inner healing and with that, some deliverance ministry along the way. There is no magic prayer bullet! Sex addiction is a sanctification process. From my counseling experience, sexual addiction is the most difficult addiction to overcome. The soul must take responsibility and endure the tribulation head on to be healed. The individual must take responsibility for his life and the sanctification journey that comes with it.

Convictions of the Holy Spirit

The Holy Spirit speaks to your heart and soul during your sanctification journey. The Holy Spirit convicts your soul of its sinful thoughts and brings your heart into the kingdom mindset of surrendering to God's will. A spiritually aligned soul will receive convictions from the Holy Spirit loud and clear.

> *"For those who are according to the flesh set their minds on the things of the flesh, but those who are according to the Spirit, the things of the Spirit. For the mind set on the flesh is death, but the mind set on the Spirit is life and peace, because the mind set on the flesh is hostile toward God; for it does not subject itself to the law of God, for it is not even able to do so, and those who are in the flesh cannot please God. However, you are not in the flesh but in the Spirit, if indeed the Spirit of God dwells in you. But if anyone does not have the Spirit of Christ, he does not belong to Him."*
> —Romans 8:5-9

The indwelling Holy Spirit is constantly at work inside you. Convictions come from sermons, reading the Word, and hearing the Holy Spirit. Faith comes from hearing.

> *"So faith comes from hearing, and hearing by the word of Christ."*
> —Romans 10:17

Immature spiritual souls will initially feel urges from their heart (spirit) that God doesn't like something about their ungodly habits. Can you remember a time when you felt the urge deep down inside to not do something? And then you went and did it regardless of the convictions of the Holy Spirit. Afterward, you felt like such a fool, or worse yet, felt ashamed for not listening! That is a conviction of the Holy Spirit. Mature, more sanctified spiritual souls will hear the Holy Spirit loudly and feel His repulsion to an act of sin the soul is contemplating committing. Mature souls strive to walk aligned in the spirit with the Holy Spirit. "But I say, walk by the Spirit, and you will not carry out the desire of the flesh. For the flesh sets its desire against the Spirit, and the Spirit against the flesh; for these are in opposition to one another, so that you may not do the things that you please. But if you are led by the Spirit, you are not under the Law" (Galatians 5:16-18).

Listening to the Holy Spirit is crucial in the soul's walk in sanctification. The deeper the union, the closer the communication between the soul and the indwelling Holy Spirit. In deliverance ministry, you will encounter people who only hear condemnation and not conviction. Voices and thoughts of condemnation are always from demonic sources. For instance, a person with a smoking addiction will hear from the Holy Spirit that he needs to stop smoking. It's not healthy to smoke and the cigarettes make him sick. That would be the tone from the Holy Spirit. A demon would say You're going to burn in the lake of fire for smoking cigarettes. God doesn't love you because of your nasty habit. The demons will also turn God's Word against you in negative ways as you study the Bible. The soul must learn to know the voice of the Shepherd and discern from other voices, such as the soul and the demonic. Immediately, when you hear condemnation in your mind, you need to identify the root source as not being from God!

In deliverance ministry you are the spiritual director; you need to discern the words coming out of the person's mouth and heart. You need to identify what words are demonic. It's simple, the demonic vocabulary is always self-condemning!

One final comment here on voices of condemnation: I have numerous testimonies of Christians who came for deliverance and just wept under the healing of the Holy Spirit. They believed the lie that God had abandoned them and that they were going to the lake of fire. The Holy Spirit overshadowed them in the prayer session and held them as their prayers for deliverance went out in tears. I was amazed to discover how many church intercessors were dealing with voices of condemnation. Change the channel and tune these voices out!

Repentance

Repentance is the changing of the heart. This eternal life-changing action is a unanimous decision by the heart and soul to discontinue in its negative behaviors and attitudes. When God gives us the gift of justification, we give Him our *new* heart. We are born again, which means we don't carry our old ways or behaviors. Again, this is much greater than a mere prayer for salvation. God's spiritual creature, which was spiritually dead and under the curse of the Law, must step out as a transformed, new spiritual being. Repentance of the heart and soul is the power that brings the transformation at justification. The most powerful evangelic saints I have ever met were former gang members and inmates. These men and women gave up the old ungodly ways of their once blackened hearts and stepped into the full power and reality of the gift of salvation. I love the evangelic atmosphere of churches made up of these kinds of saints. These people's souls completely understand the depth of their salvation.

In suburban churches, we tend to be more about the appearance at church on Sunday and less about the repentance of the heart. I was a member of this community, the frozen chosen. The pews of this church are filled with souls more worried about their fire insurance than developing a life-long, transforming relationship with Jesus. In the church of the frozen chosen, which is a mega church now in America, the congregation doesn't grasp the gift of God's grace and mercy. These souls are uncertain of their eternal salvation. How do you identify the frozen chosen? Walk up to them and ask them how certain they are about their eternity in heaven. If they answer anything less than 100 percent, then you have found yourself a frozen chosen congregation member. With these pew members, there is an interior disconnect with the indwelling Holy Spirit. Many times, the Holy Spirit is locked out of His service at the frozen chosen churches.

Pride is the preacher of the pulpit, and these people in the pews don't want to acknowledge that they need to repent. Appearance and stature in the church are more important than the salvation of the soul. In deliverance ministry, you will work with a lot of people from the church of the frozen chosen. Working with such souls requires walking them through where they are stuck in their spiritual development. You will need to help them identify obstacles to their spiritual growth they need to repent of. I am talking about spiritual direction for these souls. If the person talks to you or rebuts you more than he listens to you, he is uninterested in repenting from his sinful nature. Pray for release from working with him.

CHAPTER 4

Forgiveness

I used to teach a corporate deliverance ministry class a few years back. An interesting common thread emerged in that women who were emotionally, physically, or sexually abused by their earthly fathers couldn't connect with their heavenly Father. This emotional scar was such an inhibiting issue in the corporate deliverance session that the ministry running the classes decided the solution was to focus on delivering the individuals from an orphan spirit. Although this was part of the problem, the deliverance ministry made matters worse. After the corporate deliverance, many of the women who were experiencing childhood trauma from their fathers were stirred up even worse after the retreat. The real issue wasn't the orphan spirit; the root problem was abuse. These women were severely traumatized as children by their parents. Their primary, God-given, family protector—their father—failed them. And to make matters worse, the fathers of these women were the perpetrators of heinous emotional, physical, sexual, and possibly even ritual abuse against them. These women were carrying huge emotional detachment issues. Childhood detachment needs inner healing and not deliverance ministry. The wounds these women carried were so deep that it was difficult even to define a starting point for their healing. It's common for a broken soul, possibly even a severely fractured soul (referring to dissociative identity disorder), to seek deliverance from this horrible trauma they experienced in life; but deliverance won't work. As I stated earlier, the darker the offense and wounds, the worse off they'll be after the ministry session.

An inexperienced deliverance minister will try brute force forgiveness. Deliverance prayer ministers will lead the person through some forgiveness prayers. Angry and fractured (dissociated) human parts will surface that the minister will mistake as demonic spirits. In deliverance ministry, releasing forgiveness is beneficial in expelling demons. In inner healing, forgiveness is a very long walk with Jesus, uphill. How long does the walk take? The answer always is: as long as it takes. Days, weeks, months, years. In my experience with severe trauma, the answer is usually years.

When dealing with soul wounds or severe trauma, prematurely releasing forgiveness can be detrimental to the healing process. Yes, the Bible says we are to forgive seventy times seven, but I believe Jesus was referring to a typical offense against an individual. With a soul wound, the enemy tries to destroy a soul's salvation through severe trauma. Jesus will come alongside in inner healing ministry and walk the soul to its healing. Jesus heals the brokenhearted and He sets the captives free. What I observed through deliverance ministry is that the corporate church doesn't have a true grasp or understanding of how to lead the severely traumatized through forgiveness.

Back in 2012, I attended the Roman Catholic Southern California Renewal Communities (SCRC) conference on exorcism. One of the lecturers was an exorcist from the Chicago archdiocese named Father Jeff Grob. Fr Grob gave a very illuminating take on forgiveness that resonated with what I witnessed in my ministry sessions. I took meticulous notes, and I have since rehashed his talk on more than one occasion. Several years back M16 Ministires held monthly deliverance and healing prayer sessions at my old church, called Miracles and Warfare. There was a lot of good information in Fr Grob's talk that people attending Miracles and Warfare absolutely loved. Some years later, my presentation and notes have evolved. But the basis of this discussion has roots in what Fr Grob presented at that SCRC conference on exorcism. I now use this information in counseling sessions with people who are severely traumatized.

The necessity of releasing forgiveness first requires that an individual had an offense committed against him. In legal terms, we would define the person who received the offense a victim. An offense can be minor or it can be traumatic. Through a hardened heart or severe trauma, a soul may choose not to forgive an offender. When the soul chooses not to forgive, it is in a state of unforgiveness. Unforgiveness is an obsessive state of negative emotions of ill will against the violator. Souls in this state can be stuck and not desire to seek to release the offender from the violation. When the soul is stuck in a state of vengeful anger or a state of victimhood, it is not moving forward in healing. A soul that chooses to forgive begins to move forward in its healing process.

The following list is from Father Grob's lecture. I have added my comments to this list over the years. I call this list "The Dynamics of Forgiveness." Fr Grob's talk helps illustrate the complexities of the soul as it tries to arrive at a place where it can release forgiveness to an offender. These are the conditions the minister and the prayer recipient must understand to prepare for releasing forgiveness.

The Dynamics of Forgiveness

Forgiveness is not forgetting what happened to you. The faculties of the soul do not magically forget the offense. There is a clear awareness of the offense committed and the desire to move forward with inner healing.

1. Forgiveness is not being in denial to your traumatic experiences The soul must recognize the offense and the heart must deal with the resulting suffering. The soul has certainty that the offense committed against it was real and not imagined. The offense actually happened.

2. Forgiveness requires more than just willpower of the soul. Choosing to heal is a step to receive healing. A false deliverance ministry doctrine is that the heart instantaneously heals. Inner healing is a process that takes time. Jesus knows how long it will take for an individual to heal. Healing takes as long as it takes.

3. Forgiveness can't be given on demand from a wounded heart. The soul can't be forced to forgive. Forgiveness is an act of will of the soul and is released from the heart.
4. Forgiveness is not a magical do-over button.
5. Forgiveness does not restore a relationship back to where it was before the offense.
6. Forgiveness moves the heart and soul into the process of healing.
7. Forgiveness does not mean giving up one's right for seeking justice.
8. Forgiveness does not mean abandoning justice. There are consequences for people's actions.
9. Forgiveness does not mean excusing the offender. It's not an absolution of the offense. Nor do you have to restore any contact or relationship with the offender to forgive.
10. Forgiveness does not demonstrate moral superiority. It does not mean you're better than the offender. Forgiveness demonstrates strength from the heart and the will of the soul. Forgiveness helps restore the damaged inner dignity.
11. Forgiveness does not mean leaving it all for God. God is not the only component at work. There is the issue of the emotional wounds the offender may have left inside the heart. As the heart heals and memories or offensive thoughts surface, the soul must work under God's grace and mercy when these arise. Healing and forgiveness is a journey (sanctification).

Ministering to Forgiveness

When you are ministering forgiveness, you must discern if the individual's heart and soul are ready for this step. Some trauma is so severe that the individual you are ministering to may be considered a survivor. The trauma was life threatening, or it was overwhelming emotional abuse. If the individual experienced the trauma as a child, he might have dissociative identity disorder, and the trauma perpetrator was one or both of his parents.

To start ministering forgiveness, you must be certain that the offensive or traumatic action has stopped. The person must be in a safe place emotionally and physically. If he is in this place, the first step is for the individual is to recognize his pain. A survivor of severe trauma must understand that he has permission to hurt. The revelation of trauma does not give him permission to feel sorry for himself. It allows his soul to give the heart permission to feel pain. Many times the heart will want to remain numb. A healthy process for the heart to express pain is for the individual to share his pain with a prayer minister or a Christian counselor. As the ministry recipient shares his emotions, his soul and heart's feelings are no longer internalized. The pain is no longer compartmentalized. Through this process, the soul must clearly identify and express for itself what happened. It removes the sense of denial and allows the soul to process memories and emotions.

All of this ministry is under the grace and mercy of Jesus Christ. There is no process to this ministry. The minister follows in step with what he sees Jesus do in the session. Each person has a unique soul and each session is equally as different. Keep in mind: just because something worked for one person doesn't mean it's going to work for the next. God knows how to heal His kids. Remember, Jesus heals the brokenhearted; we're just an instrument for bringing Jesus into the session. In these sessions, I always minister with Jesus present. I don't answer questions for the individuals. I have the soul connect with the indwelling Jesus and have their soul and the Holy Spirit talk to each other. My job as a minister is to keep the soul connected to the indwelling Jesus for these sessions. I don't answer any questions regarding forgiveness of individuals. I direct all questions regarding forgiveness to the wounded soul and have them ask the indwelling Jesus in person. In nearly all sessions, it's dialogue between the two and I stay out of it. My job is to provide spiritual direction once the meeting in the soul has completed.

Before the forgiveness can be released, the wounded heart must realize that it has the right to be angry and upset for the offense. The heart and soul may also be upset at Jesus for allowing this to happen to them. The soul will gravitate to a desire for revenge. Revenge is human nature;

this is a natural emotion. The sense of revenge brings a sense of truth that the incident(s) occurred. It confronts thoughts of denial that the offense(s) actually occurred. However, we don't act on the emotions of revenge. We have the soul connect with Jesus, even if it is extremely angry at Him. He is big enough to take harsh words and then heal the broken heart of his child.

Initially, the ministry must focus on understanding the offense that occurred. You must minister and help the individual express his anger or pain. Help the soul you are pastoring understand that the pain and negative emotion doesn't define him. Perhaps he is angry at God for allowing the trauma to happen. Help the wounded heart understand the pain for what it is. Help guide the soul from a trapped victim mindset to being one of a fighting survivor. The soul begins to heal as its identity gets restored. The individual has an identity from Jesus Christ, and the traumatic wounded self is not his identity.

Gauge where the heart and soul are at in their healing. If the healing process is slow, let it be slow. Don't exasperate the wounded heart and soul. Fall in tune to the pace of Jesus and how He is bringing healing. When a wounded soul embraces forgiveness, he will be able to forgive the offender first, and later accept that God forgives him for harboring an offense. However, the hardest thing for the soul to do is to forgive itself. Unforgiveness of self is where the demonic voices will bring torment to the heart and soul trying to heal. The soul will hear internal voices of condemnation. He may also read nothing but condemnation as he reads the Bible. The prayer minister should work with the individual in teaching him to shut down these internal spiritual locutions.

In prayer or counseling sessions, just work with these things as they arise. Never push the healing, let Jesus lead. If the wound has been open for years, it may take a while for the wound to heal fully. It is Jesus that heals the wound and not the minister.

Concluding Thoughts on Forgiveness

The most important thing for a prayer minister to learn is that there is no set process for this. I used to collect prayers for this and prayers for that. What I was doing was catering to my lack of faith that I needed to do something to bring healing. You only need to show up to the session and listen to what the person is saying. Let the Holy Spirit bring revelation on what is going on. If this is a simple deliverance forgiveness issue, from a non-traumatic offense, then walk the person through repentance and some forgiveness prayers. The Holy Spirit will help you with what to say.

If you are in a ministry session and the forgiveness issue is complicated, the prayer recipient will let you know. Listen to what he is telling you and listen to what the Holy Spirit is telling you. If there is an issue with the prayer recipient releasing forgiveness, ask Jesus to give you revelation on what is going on. Is this a heart wound with diseased attitudes, or is this person a survivor of trauma? Either way, just have the faith of a mustard seed. Jesus will bring healing to those that seek it.

CHAPTER 5

Spiritual Authority in Christ

Spiritual authority is one of those subjects that isn't really taught in seminary school. The academic side of spiritual authority is presented, but not the side that relates to its application in the trenches. In 2012, I attended a conference on Roman Catholic exorcism in Anaheim, California. The most interesting revelation from this conference was from the priests in response to the spiritual warfare material presented by the Roman Catholic exorcists. The clergy in attendance had never seen or heard anything like the information presented to them, not in the seminary or in any special training. Lack of pastoral preparation for spiritual warfare in any denomination is a huge issue.

Another problem with Christians grasping the subject matter of spiritual authority is that they fear it. Most Christians fear to step into the authority Jesus gave them at the cross. We can't fear the victory we walk in. Demons are walking this earth, and when we encounter them, we are to expel them. Our natural is the supernatural in this existence.

Lack of proper training in operating in spiritual authority also creates a vacuum, sucking in those who think they know what they're doing. These individuals are well-versed in popular books and media but have never cast out a spirit. Many times, these inexperienced deliverance ministers bring more damage than healing. Even worse, these inexperienced deliverance ministers bring curses upon themselves, their families, churches, finances, and health.

Most Christians want to be experts on spiritual warfare, but when they step into battle with their book-acquired information, they tend to find out how ill-prepared they are for combat. Being unprepared leads to extreme frustration, for both the unseasoned minister and the person seeking the prayer ministry. Lack of confidence in ministry brings doubt into your faith, and you come to believe you don't have the authority to cast out spirits. Keep in mind, you are battling eternal spirit beings who have been in existence before Adam and Eve. The forces of darkness clearly understand our nature and how to defeat us. The spirits know exactly, from history, how easily we stumble in our God-given authority.

Compounding this problem are churches that build doctrines around their perceived versions of spiritual authority. The result of this is spiritual warfare battle plans that are nothing more than religious legalism. Legalism won't expel a demon, but a person of faith walking in authority certainly will.

As an example of one ridiculous doctrine, I have repeatedly heard from students in my classes that they were told by their church leaders not to touch people manifesting. When I speak on deliverance ministry and casting out demons, I demonstrate in my equipping classes how I lay hands on people and pray. The false church doctrine was that the demons could jump into them if they touched someone manifesting. Now mind you, these are also the same students who, a few minutes prior in the class, insisted that a Christian couldn't be demonized. The church has an identity crisis with all these false doctrines.

There are a lot of other popular false teachings out there that have become doctrinal within the four walls of the church. The biggest one is that Satan was made powerless at the cross. Not true. Satan was defeated at the cross, but his powers and gifts were not revoked by God. Another false doctrine is that Satan must ask for permission to oppress a Christian, as in the book of Job, or that Satan doesn't have free rein or free will. Again not true, Satan is the prince of the air. He has set up the second heaven with his government. This dispensation is a time of diabolic collateral damage—a prelude to the rebellious angels' impending doom. During this time, the satanic angels want to destroy everything!

Biblical Foundations of Spiritual Authority

The definition of authority states that a person or an organization has control of an environment. Authority is usually associated with a governing body or a ruler. Spiritual authority is granted by a governing ruler, the kingdom of God. God sits on a throne, in His mountain, in His heavenly kingdom, and all of creation are his subjects.

God is a god of love, and He created us so He could love us. When God created man, a spiritual being embodied in flesh, He wanted to interact with man; He wanted man as his cocreator.

> "Then God said, 'Let Us make man in Our image, according to Our likeness; and let them rule (have dominion - KJV) over the fish of the sea and over the birds of the sky and over the cattle and over all the earth, and over every creeping thing that creeps on the earth'."
> —Genesis 1:26

God created us in His image so we could co-rule His creation of the earth with Him. God gave us dominion, which is the power to rule. We were created to have authority over all the earth. We were to give names to the creatures in His creation.

I spoke with Roman Catholic exorcist Father Gary Thomas on this subject, and he revealed an interesting aspect of this verse in Genesis. When God gave man the ability to name the creatures, this was an attribute of spiritual authority. Father Gary explained to me this is the reason Roman Catholics water baptize babies. This Catholic Rite of Baptism is actually a mini exorcism. When a Roman Catholic priest baptizes a baby, the child is baptized with a spiritual name. This name has significance spiritually in the kingdom of God. I am a Pentecostal minister, and our tradition is to dedicate babies to God and water baptize the person later— when the soul chooses Jesus. Both baby baptisms and dedications have significance in terms of authority in the spirit realm.

Heavenly Dominion

Long before God created the earth, He created angelic creatures that are spirits. He created these creatures to participate in ruling in his heavenly realm. These angelic creatures were given dominions, sometimes called *choirs*, which are celestial ranks of hierarchy in heaven. These angelic creatures are ranked from lowest to highest into the following nine orders: angels, archangels, principalities, powers, virtues, dominions, thrones, cherubim, and seraphim. All of these creatures, both the good and the satanic angels, all serve God. Paul's epistle to the Ephesians gives us a glimpse of the choir of the fallen satanic angels.

> *"For our struggle is not against flesh and blood, but against the (heavenly) rulers, against the powers, against the world forces of this darkness, against the spiritual forces of wickedness in the heavenly places."*
> —*Ephesians 6:12*

Man's spiritual authority does not extend into the heavenly places. Only Jesus has full authority in the heavens and over his fallen angels. Mankind was created in the middle of a heavenly conflict. War is waging between two kingdoms: God's kingdom and Satan's kingdom of darkness. Satan's angels attempted to overthrow God in a rebellion and failed miserably. The consequences of this rebellion on the satanic angel ranks are that they're to be forever separated from God with no possibility, ever, of redemption. Scripture tells us that at the end of this conflict, the fallen angels will be tossed into the lake of fire. Our universe was created in the middle of this angelic war. You can imagine the fury running through Satan's spirit when he witnessed God create man and give man dominion over the new creation of the earth. Satan, who still wants to overthrow God, was certainly lusting for this power grab of authority away from man. Satan schemed to convince Adam and Eve to rebel against God and seize their dominion. Satan clearly understood rebellion and the consequences of this action. If he could get Adam and Eve to disobey God, that would be rebellion. The wages of sin is death, and death is under the dominion of Satan. Satan probably hoped, too, that man would be given no option for redemption.

Satan's Stolen Authority

When Adam and Eve fell to the original sin in the garden of Eden, they became slaves to their sin. Their slave master was Satan. Every person ever born from Adam to the present day is born under the curse of the original sin. Satan had taken authority over the earth (stolen from Adam). When Jesus went into the wilderness and fasted for forty days, Satan offered the earthly authority back to Jesus if Jesus would bow down to him. "And he (Satan) said to Him (Jesus), 'I will give you all their authority and splendor; it has been given to me, and I can give it to anyone I want to. If you worship me, it will all be yours'" (Luke 4:6-7).

In this context, it is safe to assume that everything Satan wanted to hand over to Jesus, he presumed he owned. Jesus set him straight on who really had the authority. What's interesting in this dialog between the two is that Jesus didn't acknowledge that Satan had the authority, nor did Jesus answer Satan. Instead, He reminded Satan of his place in creation: "Jesus answered him, 'It is written, "Worship the Lord your God and serve Him only"'" (Luke 4:8).

Jesus Restores Man's Authority in Creation

Paul's epistle to the Romans explains that God had a plan for redemption for Adam and Eve, and for you and I. Jesus Christ would come to our world incarnate. He would be exposed to the same fallen world as you and me, only He would live a sinless, holy life. Jesus would become the perfect sacrifice and die in our place, for our sin, on the cross. Jesus would become the second Adam.

> "So then as through one transgression there resulted condemnation to all men, even so through one act of righteousness there resulted justification of life to all men. For as through the one man's disobedience the many were made sinners, even so through the obedience of the One the many will be made righteous."
> —Romans 5:18-19

According to Romans 5, by the law of God, the first Adam sinned and left every man born into this state of original sin. The second Adam,

Jesus, was allowed to live Adam's life in substitution and undo the transgression. This imputing of sin is why Jesus is referred to as the second Adam.

> So it is written: "The first man Adam became a living being"; the last Adam, a life-giving spirit. The spiritual did not come first, but the natural, and after that the spiritual. The first man was of the dust of the earth; the second man is of heaven. As was the earthly man, so are those who are of the earth; and as is the heavenly man, so also are those who are of heaven. And just as we have borne the image of the earthly man, so shall we bear the image of the heavenly man.

—1 Corinthians 15:45-49

Authority Revoked from Satan

When Jesus was crucified, He died and descended into hades, the netherworld of death. Before the work on the cross, the righteous did not go to heaven. They were separated from God. Everyone who ever died, from Adam up until Jesus on the cross, all went to hades.[1] In hades, the righteous lived in the paradise of Abraham's bosom and the unrighteous lived in a burning chamber called hell. We know from Scripture that paradise and hell, inside hades, were separated by a giant chasm.[2] Scripture tells us that Jesus made proclamations to the imprisoned spirits in hades.

> "For Christ also died for sins once for all, the just for the unjust, so that he might bring us to God, having been put to death in the flesh, but made alive in the spirit; in which also he went and made proclamation to the spirits now in prison."
> —1 Peter 3:19

The spirits who are bound in prison are those who died before Jesus was crucified. These were God's righteous souls—like Abraham, Moses, Joshua, the thief on the cross who died next to Jesus. Even in death, these souls were separated from God. The Scripture is the prophetic fulfillment of Isaiah 61:1: "To proclaim liberty to captives and freedom

---

1 Luke 23:43
2 Luke 16:22-24

to prisoners" (Isaiah 61:1c). The prison was paradise, Abraham's bosom, in hades. When Jesus ascended, He brought the righteous captives out of the prison of hades and into the new location of paradise in heaven. "Now this expression, 'He ascended,' what does it mean except that he also had descended into the lower parts of the earth? He who descended is Himself also He who ascended far above all the heavens, so that He might fill all things" (Ephesians 4:9-10).

The souls were brought to heaven to live out eternity in the presence of God. Jesus completed His primary objective: to remove the sins of man that separated him from everlasting life with Jesus Christ. Jesus had conquered sin and death.

> "I am the Living One; I was dead, and now look, I am alive forever and ever! And I hold the keys of death and hades."
> —Revelation 1:18

The keeper of the keys of hades was Satan. Without the covering of the blood sacrifice of Jesus Christ, the soul is a prisoner to hades. When Jesus conquered death on the cross, He also took away Satan's presumed authority over creation.

Authority Restored

Through His work on the cross, Jesus redeemed us. We were no longer separated from God, the veil was torn, and our authority and dominion over the earth was restored. When Jesus was resurrected, He spoke with His disciples.

> "And Jesus came up and spoke to them, saying, "All authority has been given to Me in heaven and on earth."
> —Matthew 28:18

Jesus never lost His heavenly authority. Satan spoke to Jesus with pride and audacity (Luke 4). As I mentioned, Satan never really had the authority over the earth. Jesus came to legally seize back the first Adam's dominion and undo the spiritual separation between God and man.

Jesus's Victory at the Cross

The miracle of the cross was the pivotal battle in the dark angelic realm's undoing. The cross had set a legal precedent in the spirit realm. The kingdom of the satanic angels had been defeated.

> *"Having canceled the charge of our legal indebtedness, which stood against us and condemned us; he has taken it away, nailing it to the cross. And having disarmed the powers and authorities, he made a public spectacle of them, triumphing over them by the cross."*
> —*Colossians 2:14-15*

The dark angelic realm's days are now numbered for their judgment. Jesus's work on the cross physically sets the dispensation in time for the start of the end-times church.

> *"But when this priest had offered for all time one sacrifice for sins, he sat down at the right hand of God, and since that time he waits for his enemies to be made his footstool."*
> —*Hebrews 10:12-13*

God clearly outlined the details of the fall of the satanic kingdom in the apostle John's book of Revelation. God's Word is complete and absolute. The enemy knows Scripture, and he knows God is immutable in His Word. When Jesus returned to heaven, He didn't leave us powerless. Our authority over creation was restored. Restoration of our dominion has spiritual significance. The low-level fallen satanic angels, which we call demons, are roaming the earth. We are cohabitants in a world that is a makeshift prison for these low-level fallen angelic beings. We have terrestrial authority over these low-level demons. To exist in this world, we must walk in our spiritual authority and have a kingdom mindset.

Your Authority from the Cross

So why aren't Christians walking in their spiritual authority? The number one issue my ministry encounters when a person is receiving deliverance prayer is that he is not standing in his own spiritual authority. This weak prayer posture leaves an open door for spirits to oppress him or for the spirit manifestation to return. Spirits always check the locks when they're evicted. Unfortunately, I have found that most people (including many Christians) just want to be delivered from their pain and not receive the true salvation Jesus gave them. Standing in authority means resisting the devil in the areas Jesus just cleaned out!

There are also the doctrinal issues within the church on spiritual authority. There is the unbiblical fear of contracting the spirit by the laying on of hands during prayer ministry. Other Christians who have never even cast out a spirit tell me how they're warring in the second heaven, which is extremely dangerous and again, unbiblical. The heavens belong to Jesus, and we are to stay out! Never go out looking for a fight with a demon. You will get what you ask for!

To learn to walk in your authority, you need to be a person of faith. God the Father is not going to reveal something to you that you are not ready to handle. When you have a solidified relationship and your soul is in union with the indwelling Jesus, you will start seeing the supernatural revealed. I am not talking about over-the-top experiences and visions. I am talking about sublime, interior encounters with the indwelling Jesus. Jesus releases these graces at His discretion. Never pay attention to what other people are experiencing. You are in your own unique and special relationship with Jesus. Follow the will of the Father in these matters and allow Him to shape you. Patience, humility, and submitting to the will of the Father are signs of a mature spiritual soul. I believe what I stated here is reflected in Luke 10:17, when the seventy new disciples went out and healed the sick and cast out demons. Through their faith, they were released into signs and wonders.

The Holy Spirit Reveals Your Authority

Now for the *ah-ha moment*! That's what I call the moment when a Christian witnesses his own spiritual authority in Jesus Christ. This encounter is a divine moment that is arranged by the Holy Spirit to demonstrate your spiritual authority firsthand. I have a particular story I like to share about a friend I worked with, Susan, who was a member of my prophetic ministry outreach team. Susan, my wife, Lisa, and I were at a corporate deliverance retreat where attendees get delivered from generational curses, strongholds, and soul ties. This retreat was a powerful, soul-liberating event where hundreds of people, from a multitude of local churches, go through prayer lines of ministers to get delivered of various oppressive spirits throughout the day. At the end of this particular day, the sin topic was cleaning up soul ties from ungodly sexual encounters. Susan and Lisa were intercessors behind one minister who was praying for a man who had been raped in prison. A demon manifested in the person receiving prayer and he started screaming. It was so loud, the hundreds of people in the large church sanctuary could all hear him. It was loud and disruptive. I was at the back of the large sanctuary doing intercession for the ministry as the man started yelling. I looked over at the ruckus and now several pastors headed over there to minister. I just stayed at my position and continued to pray for liberation. Spirits like to distract and pull people like me, who are intercessors, away from their jobs. This is a distraction to cause a break in the front lines of ministry.

As I watched the other ministers, they now entered into a shouting match with the demon. It was extremely disturbing and was distracting the deliverance of others. Rule number one of a spirit of distraction is to shut it down. These ministers were increasingly becoming part of the demonic spectacle. These ministers were appointed prayer leaders who were supposed to be seasoned in spiritual warfare. No one was binding the demon to be silent! No one! At this point, I was having a conversation with the Holy Spirit on what to do. The situation was quickly escalating into spiritual chaos. The Holy Spirit released me to go over to the spectacle and take action. It took me about a minute or two to calmly walk over to where the demoniac and the ministers were all shouting. I was about to bind the demon to silence when the Holy Spirit spoke to me. He said that He wanted my friend Susan to bind the demon. Susan was now standing just outside the small growing wall of ministers in a shouting match with the demon. I looked over at Susan, and she was praying. She saw me looking at her and returned a puzzled look. She wasn't sure what to do. This incident was the first time she had seen a demonic manifestation. I walked over to Susan and told her to look at the demon and say, "I bind you to silence! In the name of Jesus!"

She looked at me puzzled again. I nodded my head for her to say it. Susan has a very quiet voice, very soft. Even without all this shouting going on in the background, you would need to carefully listen to Susan's voice. In her gentle voice, which I couldn't hear over the ministers and the demoniac yelling, she said, "I bind you to silence! In the name of Jesus!" At that instance, the demon shut up! Susan looked at me puzzled again.

"That was all you!" I told her. "Now order it to leave!"

She did it in her soft, quiet voice. The ministers were bewildered and didn't really have a clue what had just happened. With all the shouting, they never even knew that it was Susan who bound the demon. Sadly, the men gave into their pride. They strutted around for minutes afterward believing it was of their own individual doing and because of their expertise in spiritual warfare. With all the chaos they added to the environment, it was doubtful they assisted at all in the man's liberation. Not one of them walked in the authority they thought they had. And not one of them bound the demon to silence and stopped its disruption of a deliverance retreat. A seventy-year-old woman with a soft voice, who was interceding for them, bound the demon to silence and then cast it out! That was Susan's ah-ha moment. The ah-ha moment is when you see with your own eyes the authority and power you walk in. Ah-ha moments are divine appointments arranged by the Holy Spirit for you to see the authority that you already walk in. Luke 10 is a biblical reference to an ah-ha moment. "The seventy returned with joy, saying, 'Lord, even the demons are subject to us in Your name.' And He said to them, 'I was watching Satan fall from heaven like lightning. Behold, I have given you authority to tread on serpents and scorpions, and over all the power of the enemy, and nothing will injure you. Nevertheless do not rejoice in this, that the spirits are subject to you, but rejoice that your names are recorded in heaven'" (Luke 10:17-20).

What I truly love about Susan and her testimony is how God uses the meek to bring victory.

Jesus tells us in Scripture that you should rejoice that your name is written in the Book of Life.[3] What I believe Jesus is revealing here is that we can easily obsess and go overboard with a ministry focused on casting out demons. It is more important that you develop a deep relationship with the indwelling Jesus than focus on demons. Demons are insignificant in the Bible. In fact, after the book of Acts, demons are not even mentioned at all. When they do appear in the New Testament, they're cast out. Jesus didn't seek them out, they just stumbled into his ministry and got cast out. Learn the difference here.

Fearing Your Authority

A Christian under attack will often run to other people to pray for them. By this I mean they didn't even bother to stand in their authority, they called or e-mailed out to prayer warriors for help instead. Stop outsourcing prayer! Having other people pray for you is not standing in your authority. Stand up for yourself. The demonic forces recognize this lacking in your faith and authority and press in harder. Healing author E.W. Kenyon commented on this issue as well,

> I receive letters from many faraway countries asking for prayer Why? Because the people who ask for prayer haven't confidence in their own faith. For some reason they do not believe in themselves. They do not believe in what Christ wrought for them, or what they are in Christ.[4]

When you step in your authority in warfare, the demonic will always challenge you. The forces simply don't surrender, especially to people with weak authority. Satan challenged God in heaven and led a failed rebellion. Satan challenged Adam and Eve, who had authority over the earth. Satan challenged Jesus and lost at the cross. Satan and his forces of darkness will certainly challenge you. To be a warrior, you must have a strong walk in faith with the Savior!

---

3 Luke 10:20

4 E.W. Kenyon, *Jesus the Healer* (Lynnwood: Kenyon's Gospel Publishing Society, 2004), 7.

CHAPTER 6

Strongholds

A stronghold is a military term that references a fortified structure protected from an attack. In spiritual warfare, a stronghold is a fortified belief system. The beliefs can be either righteous or ungodly. In a stronghold, the soul's will and intellect strongly defend its system of beliefs. There are good and there are bad strongholds in your soul. Your soul is the battlefield in this spiritual war.

Christ-Centered Soul

In spiritual warfare, a stronghold is considered to be something negative. Not all strongholds are demonic. We are supposed to have a stronghold in our soul that is Christ-centric. A good stronghold of the soul is one that is righteous and fortified in God's law, His will, mercy, and grace. A good spiritual stronghold is Christ-centric if the soul believes and operates in the kingdom mindset.

> "The Lord is my rock and my fortress and my deliverer, my God, my rock, in whom I take refuge; my shield and the horn of my salvation, my stronghold." —Psalm 18:2

Souls with a stronghold in Christ safeguard themselves from deceptive thoughts. A protected soul takes every thought captive. In a godly stronghold, the soul is in union with the indwelling Trinity. A soul in union with God has a deep relationship through prayer and experience with its creator, the Lord Jesus Christ. The soul strives only to carry out the will of God the Father. The soul wants to imitate the heart and soul of Jesus Christ. A healthy soul is Christ-centered. The goal of deliverance ministry is to direct the focus of the soul back onto the indwelling Jesus.

Demonic Strongholds

In an unhealthy stronghold, the soul is intensely under attack with thoughts contrary to God's will. The apostle Paul defines a demonic stronghold as arrogant thoughts that are contrary to God's thoughts for you.

> *"For though we walk in the flesh, we do not war according to the flesh, for the weapons of our warfare are not of the flesh, but divinely powerful for the destruction of fortresses. We are destroying speculations and every lofty thing raised up against the knowledge of God, and we are taking every thought captive to the obedience of Christ, and we are ready to punish all disobedience, whenever your obedience is complete"*
> *—2 Corinthians 10:3-6*

In this Scripture, the apostle Paul told us that the battlefield is the mind. The war is not of the flesh but of the soul. A Christ-centered soul can tear down and prevent the building of strongholds. Demonic strongholds consist of speculations, unconfirmed rumors, and lofty ideas, which are prideful self-elevated thoughts. Where have we seen this before? Lucifer! Demons have access to the faculties of the mind and they can insert speculations. Ever have a strange feeling at your workplace that there was a conspiracy against you? And it turned out not to be true. Ever wondered how those thoughts got inside your head? Your intellect was the recipient of a demonic lie.

Lofty thoughts revolve around one's exaggerated self-importance. These arrogant thoughts fuel the fire of temptation. The crafty serpent in the garden of Eden tempted Adam and Eve to eat from the Tree of Knowledge of Good and Evil. What the serpent presented to Adam and Eve were deceptions of reasoning that affected the intellect of their souls.

When deception seeps into your soul, your intellect is tempted to reason against God. These thoughts of self-importance can, after a while, fabricate a darker belief system that runs contrary to God's will. An ungodly belief system is all the thoughts you have that are contrary to God's thoughts for you. Leanne Payne calls these ungodly beliefs, diseased attitudes.[1] These deeply ingrained ideas and behaviors go against everything God believes to be true for you.

When your soul becomes self-important, it is no longer Christ-centered. You become consumed in the lies of the enemy rather than in the rest and peace of the truth of Jesus Christ. Be aware, too, that these self-centered attitudes can also come from pain and trauma rather than from exaggerated thoughts of self-importance. Again, in ministry sessions, discern what is going on with the soul in front of you.

Demonic strongholds come up frequently as a topic of spiritual warfare. These diseased mindsets surface many times in deliverance ministry sessions. Although the roots of these are demonic, they can also be an inner healing issue. The demonic is present because it has rooted itself in a traumatic emotion or an ungodly belief system that has become a diseased attitude of the soul. Deliverance ministry sessions can tackle some inner healing issues. Darker rooted pain from trauma requires focused inner healing prayer ministry. It could take years for the soul and Jesus to walk together through a complete healing. A gentle deliverance usually follows the completed inner healing. By this I mean the wounded portion of the soul fully surrenders to Jesus. With the miracle of the healing comes the expulsion of the demonic oppression.

Guilt, Shame, and Self-Hatred

A soul that is in union with God fears to offend God because it knows it will suffer the consequences of committing sin. The soul must take thoughts captive and squash the urges of temptation as they surface in the mind. When the soul fails to be obedient and it caves to a thought of

---

1 Leanne Payne, *Restoring the Christian Soul* (Grand Rapids: Zondervan, 2006), 27.

temptation, it will act out and commit sin. The soul will not openly repent for some acts of sin, such as sexual promiscuity.

When the Christian soul is experiencing guilt and shame, it is no longer Christ-centered. Trauma has rooted itself in the soul, and the demonic speak into this wound. These speculations become diseased attitudes with destructive demonic intentions to drive the person to self-hatred and eventually harm themselves. At this point, the demonic have lied repetitiously that the soul is unworthy of being saved. The soul is overwhelmed with thoughts of anger, self-hatred, regret, embarrassment, and riddled with overwhelming guilt. Help comes in the form of Jesus restoring the soul.

Let's look at an example where a child grew up in the home of an alcoholic father. In this environment, the child was subjugated to emotional, physical, and possibly sexual abuse. The repeated severe trauma created what is called a soul wound. The soul wound is a deep emotional memory that is a stronghold of inner pain.

In most cases like this, the child may even have a deeper darker stronghold of dissociation and develop multiple identities. The demons will ruthlessly bombard the faculties of these souls with messages of condemnation, guilt, and shame. This demonic chatter is overwhelming, and it becomes a diseased attitude of the intellect of self-hatred and failure. The power of this is so strong that children surviving this trauma are seldom able to connect with the heavenly Father in prayer. A stronghold of emotional pain exists where traumatic memories of the earthly father prevent the soul from connecting to the heavenly Father. As I mentioned in the chapter on forgiveness, many corporate deliverance ministries have addressed this as a deliverance issue. This ministry approach is ill-advised for survivors of emotional trauma. The deep emotional wounds go beyond the scope of corporate deliverance ministry. These strongholds require patience and timing to heal. They can take a magnitude of years to heal in the adult life as God and Christian counselors address the individual's identity and his identity in Jesus Christ. When Jesus heals the emotional wound, He also expels the demons. It is a much gentler deliverance. Depending on the process of healing, deliverance may or may not be required. It all depends on what surfaces during the walk with Jesus and His timing in healing.

Free Will Soul Ties

In deliverance ministry, many people associate soul ties to sexual relationships. Soul ties can be sexual in origin, but it is not the complete story. Keep in mind that soul ties can be godly or ungodly, and they don't necessarily have to be sexual in nature.

A soul tie is a bonding of the soul's will to another person through relationship. We can have godly and healthy freewill soul ties with the indwelling Trinity. Our soul is said to be in union with Jesus Christ. We can have healthy willful soul ties to our spouse, both sexual and relationship wise, through covenant. We have healthy relationship soul ties with our children. We also have healthy soul ties with friends and relatives. We can have a covenant relationship with people in our lives. Covenants are spiritual in nature, just as we are in a spiritual covenant with God. In these relationships, our soul picks up attributes from the other souls we interact with throughout our lives. A soul tie is a connection our soul freely accepts from another person.

Unhealthy soul ties come from free-will bonds of the soul that are ungodly and bring with them ungodly belief systems. The most common unhealthy willful soul tie is the act of sexual union out of wedlock. Whether this is premarital, adultery, promiscuity, and unfortunately even rape, the act of sexuality is spiritual when the flesh becomes one in the union.

> "Now Dinah the daughter of Leah, whom she had borne to Jacob, went out to visit the daughters of the land. When Shechem the son of Hamor the Hivite, the prince of the land, saw her, he took her and lay with her by force. He was deeply attracted to Dinah the daughter of Jacob, and he loved the girl and spoke tenderly to her."
> -Genesis 34:1-3

This Scripture depicts the sexual violation of Leah's daughter, Dinah. In verse 3, Shechem became deeply attracted to her, his will bonded with the woman he had forced himself upon. There was a spiritual connection and transference between the two, an unhealthy covenant that was made through an ungodly sexual union. The soul must repent of and renounce this act. Many times these sexual soul ties are the root of sexual strongholds of guilt and shame.

As two flesh join and a spiritual union occurs, the soul also takes on the spirits and curses of the other person. This spreading of curses and spirits is why most witches are promiscuous; they know they can spread and receive demons through sex. Consider this point about sleeping with promiscuous people: you pick up all the spirits they received. The math on this can be exponential, even though you may have only had a single moment of weakness.

Unhealthy soul ties are also made non-sexually through those who educate us and nourish us spiritually. You could have a bad soul tie with someone you looked up to at church and found out he was living a double lifestyle. Recently, I worked with young lady, named Tammy, who formed a strange free will bond by allowing a person to pray for her. Tammy, was a prophetic minister who met a guy at a conference and felt a connection with him. This whole interaction was completely innocent. Tammy had this individual pray over her, and later she felt like she got slimed by something spiritual. Tammy knew right away there was something wrong spiritually about the guy who had prayed over her. I worked with Tammy, and during a single prayer session we broke off the soul ties.

When I do curse breaking with psychics, card readers, and members of the occult, I have the people repent and renounce the freewill soul ties with the people who mentored them. In occult ritual abuse, this goes one step further: one of the fractured identities is an imprint of the mind control programmer. The programmer imprint won't go away with soul tie breaking, it requires lengthy work in healing the identity and leading him to Jesus Christ.

A prayer for breaking free-will soul ties is provided here. This prayer should be used in a prayer ministry session and not read alone. Many people I work with in prayer sessions don't want to do this because they say they've already read it. I ask them if they read the prayer with another minister present, and their response is usually no, they read it from my book, *A Field Guide to Spiritual Warfare*. Just reading it to yourself in a book for soul tie breaking is ineffective.

Soul tie breaking is a matter of public (within the confines of the prayer team) renunciation and proclamation. There is power in breaking soul ties through confession and renunciation.

Prayer for Renouncing Soul Ties

Heavenly Father, I thank you for loving me. I confess my sin of being sexually impure and worldly. I ask for your forgiveness of my sexual promiscuity. I repent of my own sexual sins and of the soul ties I received through these sins.

I take ownership of my family line, in the past and the future. I renounce and break all soul ties from my body. I renounce Satan's hold on me through these impure acts. I also renounce ties to witchcraft. In Jesus's name, I ask you to release me from all unclean spirits that I received. In Jesus's name, I also ask you to remove all unclean spirits from my children. Release me, my family, and my future generations from the spirits of perversion, the occult, and religion.

From this day forward I want to live blessed under the covering of the blood of Jesus Christ. I pray this in your precious name. Amen.

Ungodly Belief Systems and Diseased Attitudes

Ungodly belief systems are the building material of strongholds and soul hurts. A system of ungodly beliefs corrupts the will and intellect with diseased attitudes. These diseased attitudes can include hopelessness, depression, believing you'll never be able to be healed from pornographic or drug addiction, and so forth. These are diseased attitudes because the soul is sick inside with these false beliefs about itself. Diseased attitudes are the number one reason you conduct an interview with the prayer recipients before initiating prayer ministry. Get a feel for what is really going on. Their diseased attitudes will tell you one story and your notetaking of their ungodly beliefs about themselves will reveal the truth.

When working with souls that have dissociative identity disorder (DID), you may find yourself going in circles in deliverance ministry. A ministry session spinning its wheels in the mud may be an indicator of DID. You can be ministering to a person and then suddenly he tells you he is going to hell for smoking, as an example. This notion comes in completely sideways in the ministry, and your ministry team is all looking at each other a bit confused. There is no rhyme or reason as to why the ministry conversation jumped to this point. It's a diseased attitude that randomly surfaces. It makes no sense to what is going on currently in the ministry session. After a few minutes, you may get the person to move on past this in ministry and then wham! You're back to square one with him believing he is going to hell for smoking cigarettes. This revolving door memory condition is a classic example of working with someone who is DID, and he thinks the voices in his head are demonic. Well, maybe a few are, but the committee in the head is made up of fractured human parts. You must identify if the source is demonic or a broken person, and you must exercise true spiritual discernment!

The interview process is everything! Capture all the ungodly beliefs the people say about themselves. Many times, the words out of their mouths systematically reveal their real stronghold. If you can multitask, start asking the Holy Spirit for Scripture that reveals the truth about who they are for each diseased attitude they have revealed about themselves. When the interview is over, review the ungodly beliefs you wrote down in your notes. Have them write down the truth that the Holy Spirit is telling them about themselves. Typically, in ungodly belief systems and the breaking down of these strongholds, deliverance comes through heavy deep tears. If they're crying in their revelation, then the Holy Spirit is overshadowing them and delivering them. Always be attentive to what the Holy Spirit is doing in the session.

Prayer for Breaking Ungodly Thoughts

Jesus, please forgive me for believing thoughts that are contrary to those you have for me. I know my ungodly thoughts do not identify who I am in you. Please forgive me for believing the lie that _____.

I renounce those thoughts about myself, and I repent for the behavior that has entered me from listening to them. Jesus, please reveal the other thoughts that are contrary to the truth that you see in me.

Jesus, please forgive me.

During the prayer session, ministers should listen to the Holy Spirit for the truth He is speaking about the injured soul. Refrain from prophetic ministry; just listen for the truth the Holy Spirit is sharing. Listen for Scripture the Holy Spirit leads you to that tells who this person is in Jesus Christ. After the session, give the person goals for life to build these truths into his life.

CHAPTER 7

Hearing God and Prophetic Ministry

Whenever dealing with afflicted souls, deliverance ministers many times encounter brick walls built up of lies from the enemy that the prayer recipient believes to be inner truths. These are the brick and mortar of strongholds. Spiritual truth and revelation from Jesus tear down these diabolic strongholds. The purpose of deliverance ministry is to restore the focus of the prayer recipient's soul back on Jesus. The prophetic gifts can be very powerful in bringing down strongholds and diseased attitudes. The walls may seem impenetrable, but the truth may trickle into the session in the form of prophetic words of knowledge. Prophetic ministry is when God supernaturally intervenes in the ministry session and speaks truth through His ministers to the prayer recipient.

When I mention prophetic ministry, I am talking about New Testament prophecy similar to that found in Paul's epistle to the Corinthians.[1] New Testament prophetic ministry is about hearing from God. Many times, God will speak to everyone in the session at the same time, both to the ministers and the recipient, as a means of confirmation that the message is coming from God. I used the term "trickle" to make a point that

---

1 1 Corinthians 14:1-5

hearing God during ministry is very subtle. God doesn't come crashing into the eye of our soul, the reception center for God's communication in us, sounding like Charlton Heston or with a voice of thunder. Well, maybe for you He might. For me, the voice is very subtle and gentle. The majority of the people I have worked with who are legitimately prophetic have all confirmed that the voice of God is almost sublime, very subtle. It's never a "so sayeth the Lord" voice. The Holy Spirit is in union with the prayer minister's soul. The Holy Spirit may speak using the minister's own voice of consciousness. There are pros and cons to this form of supernatural communication, which is not clairvoyance or channeling. I am speaking of mental prayer, where there is bi-directional communication with God the creator. Prayer is how we communicate with the triune God. When your soul is in union with God, you can hear his voice. "My sheep hear My voice, and I know them, and they follow Me" (John 10:27).

The justified believer's heart becomes the new temple where the Holy Spirit dwells.[2] We have direct access to the Holy Spirit through prayer and mental conversation. The pros are that each and every believer has the same direct access to the Holy Spirit as the pope, Billy Graham, the late Kathryn Kuhlman, and even the apostles of the Gospels. When you have reached a maturity in your prayer life and have daily conversations with the indwelling Trinity, you learn to know his voice. It's simply a matter of fact in your prayer walk and spiritual growth. God, the superior Trinity, created us in His image, but we differ from our creator in that we are spiritual creatures of flesh, soul, and spirit. And we are the inferior trinity. God created us in His image so we could commune with Him through prayer.

Locutions

The cons of hearing God, as brilliantly outlined by the Roman Catholic mystic Saint Teresa of Avila, is that we, the recipients, are fallible. The classics on mystical theology (the study of how God interacts with us

---

2 1 Corinthians 3:16

through our prayers) call the church mystics' ability to hear God, or a the voice of a spirit, a locution.

Saint Teresa of Avila defined primary sources we hear locutions from: our own soul, angels—both God's messengers and satanic angels, and God. When we learn to hear from God, our own soul can get zealous and make stuff up. By this I mean God may take a while to answer our petitions, but instead of waiting for a response, the soul will fabricate what it wants to hear back from God. When learning to hear from God, we must purge ourselves of instant gratification and learn to wait on the Lord for his answers in prayer. We can also hear locutions from the angelic—both God's messengers and the demonic. Rarely does God send his messengers to interact with us. Many people I have worked with who claimed they were receiving angelic messages or having conversations with angels were doing so with masquerading angels of light. I highly recommend not engaging or requesting (in prayer) to communicate with or to see angels. The heavens belong to Jesus and we are to stay out of them. How did I know these were masquerading angels of light speaking to these individuals? The messages were always condescending and full of words of condemnation. Or they were revelations of angelic messengers bringing visions of hell. There are a small handful of people I know of who do interact with angels, and what is going on there is from God. How do I know? The message is biblically sound, and the effort is for kingdom building. Again, this is extremely rare!

One key thing about the people I worked with who were speaking to false angels of light is that they were receiving false and blasphemous prophecies about the church and the kingdom of Jesus Christ. These people were all on the verge of being strapped down on a gurney in county general hospital from their obsession with these demonic locutions.

By learning to be patient, God teaches us how to hear from Him and gives us the respect we need to approach Him in prayer and with petitions. Over time we learn how to wait on the Lord and respect His timing. How long does it take to hear from the Lord? However long He wants it to take. Each and every one of us learning to hear from God knows that the first lessons are in patience and operating in humility. As the soul learns to hear from God, the soul deepens in its relationship with him. Learning to hear from the indwelling God is a part of our transforming union. Through this process of sanctification of the soul, the transforming union, the soul learns to hear His voice. Sadly, I have worked with some people who professed themselves to be prophetic and yet couldn't connect with God at all in their own prayer lives. The inability for the soul to connect with God becomes evident rather quickly in prayer ministry sessions.

One of the downfalls of hearing God today is that we outsource our prophetic ministry to prophetic ministers. In other words, rather than going through prayer and supplication (being face down on the carpet and praying to Jesus), our human soul is a bit lazy and would rather have a prophetic minister speak to God for us. I always found this disheartening. God tore the veil of the temple so we could have direct access to Him. Don't be like other souls that have allowed themselves to fall into the deception that prophetic ministers can hear from God better than you can. Can you see the dilemma here? The same Holy Spirit is in you that is in the prophetic ministers. The same curse of the original sin is in them as is in you. Just because you haven't received the answer you wanted from God doesn't mean you're going to hear it from a prophetic speaker. I don't seek prophetic words about myself or my ministry. I hear from God by being patient and humble; God speaks to me as I am obedient to His protocols. He is the creator of the universe, Lord of Lords, and King of Kings.

I have seen firsthand too much abuse of the prophetic ministry, as the present church perceives it. We have lately turned it into something it isn't. The purpose of prophetic ministry is to edify the church body and to build the kingdom. Instead, we are using it for, "*God, tell me something about myself!*" I used to run a Friday night homeless street ministry in San Francisco called Night Strike. We would go on the streets and minister to the homeless, drug addicts, and prostitutes. Using prophetic ministry, we would give souls we encountered on the streets a touch from their heavenly Father. It was a powerful ministry, and we witnessed lots of miracles, deliverances, and miraculous healing on those streets. Do you want to know when the lowest Night Strike turnouts for our ministers were? Whenever a church in the area held a prophetic conference, I would lose a majority of my non-regular team members. These individuals decided receiving a prophetic word for themselves from God at a conference was more important than ministering to the poor and the sick on the streets. Jesus, when were you hungry? Jesus, when did you need clothes?

I don't go to church services seeking prophetic words. When God wants to tell me something, He talks to me directly or He sends some-one to get my attention. I have close friends who are the most amazing, 1 Corinthians 14, prophetic ministers -you've never heard of nor ever will. They aren't self-seeking or self-promoting. Sometimes God will send a message to me through them. My favorite is when God sends kids to give me a prophetic word. God always catches me off guard when He uses someone to send me a word from Him. Just recently, I was visiting a church in which my daughter-in-law sings on the worship team. While in the church service, my mind was pondering and calculating how to raise money for counseling scholarships for a couple of ritually abused women that needed my help. I was frustrated I couldn't raise the money on my own. When the church service was over, a woman I used to work with who was a ritual survivor came up to me. I thought she came over to say hi to me. The part that was up in her didn't recognize me. Her pre-senter that was up had never met me. This happens a lot with DID. She approached me and told me that she had a prophetic word for me. Get this, her word was that I needed to "stop reasoning about finances and just let the Holy Spirit do all the work." What timing? God used a ritual abuse survivor to send me a prophetic word. Even though the woman's primary core presenter wasn't up, she could still hear from God. And sending a ritual abuse survivor to deliver his message is totally from God. It is times like these when I know I don't need to seek out a prophetic word. God will always speak to me one way or another.

For my ministry needs, my direct communication with God is suf-ficient. The most important prophetic minister is you, and it is all based on developing an intimate relationship with the indwelling Jesus in your heart (his temple). Don't misread what I am saying here. I don't get answers right away for things I am praying about. Hearing from God means sometimes months of not receiving an answer, or any answer at all, for that matter. Many times God answers in the form of life direction and Holy Spirit urges that I believe are not even associated to what I am asking for. God sees the big picture that I don't.

Learning to Move in the Prophetic

The best way to learn to operate in the prophetic is to spend lots of time with God and pray into this. First and foremost, make sure you can connect with God during your Scripture meditations and prayer time. This form of meditation doesn't mean you have to memorize Scripture. It means to let the Word permeate your consciousness as you read and let the Holy Spirit unpack it. When you can connect to God through this, you will begin to hear His internal voice more clearly. You connect with God by having daily mental prayer conversations with Him. Let the Holy Spirit train you. The Holy Spirit is the best teacher, and you can learn to rely on Him for your instruction.

There are also some great Holy Spirit-based equipping courses available. I am a fan of Streams Ministries by the late John Paul Jackson. Youtube.com has videos by John Paul Jackson, and his excellent course "The Art of Hearing God" is available on that site. John Paul Jackson's teachings are also available as online classes from his site, streamsministries. com. For my outreach event ministers, this course is a prerequisite. I can't recommend this course enough! What I really like about John Paul Jackson's course is that he teaches the importance of the character of the minister and his identity in Jesus Christ.

When Jesus used prophetic evangelism with the woman at the well (John 4), He exercised His complete compassion for the individual He was trying to reach. Bringing Jesus's compassion into every prophetic ministry session is critical. Prophetic ministry is a powerful spiritual tool for inner healing and deliverance.

There is a tremendous responsibility on the minister to operate in humility and to live a life that's in a transforming union with Jesus Christ. The minister must be repentant, work wholeheartedly on his own sanctification, and walk in a relationship with Jesus Christ. An unrepentant minister living in sin will be an unsuccessful minister and will find himself inevitably sidelined by the Holy Spirit. A minister may have a powerful gift from God, but if he's not walking with God, God will bench him. I have worked with ministers who would not take correction in using their gift. Not taking advice and correction from these Holy Spirit-sent mentors is operating in pride. Sometimes a minister will behave like this because he's trying to hide his sin. Sadly, the sin in his soul is overshadowing the voice of the indwelling Holy Spirit. Therefore, everything this person thinks he's hearing from God is actually coming from his soul. Seasoned ministers will discern this and catch it in a heartbeat. Many are called but few are chosen.

Modern day prophetic ministry is stigmatized because too many ministers misinterpret the role of the New Testament prophet. Prophetic ministry means you can hear the internal voice of God. Hearing a prophetic word doesn't mean you're a prophet. The last prophet was John the Baptist. I believe there are no more prophets. That was strictly Old Testament. The difference is that the Old Testament prophet heard directly from the Holy Spirit. The New Testament prophet perceives from the Holy Spirit. Note the difference in the prophetic styles of receiving versus perceiving. The sole purpose for end-times church prophecy is to build up a person with a positive affirmation. We don't give negative words or prophesy that people are going to be sick, or have a baby, or anything extreme. In ministry outreach environments, we don't correct or rebuke the lifestyle of the individual receiving the word from God. We let the encounter with the Holy Spirit speak to the person's heart. The Holy Spirit knows exactly what to say for the encounter.

Discerning God's Voice

Listening to God is a mystical experience. Mystical means God is mysterious. He operates in His own ways. You can hear God because your body is the temple of the Holy Spirit; you carry God inside you.

If you are just starting out in prophetic ministry, how can you tell if a message is from God? Keep in mind that hearing from God is very subtle.

Many times, a thought or a picture will drop into your mind that is in no way anything you were thinking of before the experience. This dropping in of a picture or a word is the beginning of a mystical locution. It is so subtle that you may have experienced this and not caught it. If you think you are getting a locution, you are hearing God. Ask the Holy Spirit about what you think you're perceiving.

God will build you up as his prophetic messenger. You may start to receive one or two different kinds of messages—a word of exhortation or a word of condemnation. Remember, we are to build up, encourage, and come alongside. God does not want us to tear down the people we are ministering to, especially if they are in bondage or have a severely broken heart. God will exhort with a good message whereas Satan will give a bad message of condemnation. Jesus=good and the devil=bad is the premise for filtering locutions. Always test the spirits and see if what you're receiving lines up biblically.

> "Beloved, do not believe every spirit, but test the spirits to see whether they are from God, because many false prophets have gone out into the world. "
> -1 John 4:1

To learn prophetic ministry, spend time with God and understand how your prophetic gift works. We are all unique, and God gives us all radically different types of spiritual gifts. Do you hear or see from God? My prophetic gift is that I am a seer. I perceive pictures from the Holy Spirit. I don't always understand what He is showing me, and I must pray to unpack the message. When I do outreaches, I bring a sketchbook and colored pencils and sketch what I see. There are times when the recipients see what I am sketching and they already know what the message from God is. It's a very personal message, and I don't have to interpret what God is conveying. I know other people who are prophetic singers: God gives them a song to sing over the ministry recipient. I have even witnessed a prophetic dancer deliver a person from unclean spirits through her dance. That was a mind-blowing experience. Utilize what God put inside of you to use. Take time to understand your gift and most important, know your identity in Jesus Christ.

A Word on Old Testament False Prophecy

But what about false prophecy? What if you get random mental gibberish? Isn't it a sin punishable by death if you get a soulish message? Yes, if you were an Old Testament prophet sent by God.

> *"I will raise up a prophet from among their countrymen like you, and I will put My words in his mouth, and he shall speak to them all that I command him" (Deuteronomy 18:18). "But the prophet who speaks a word presumptuously in My name which I have not commanded him to speak, or which he speaks in the name of other gods, that prophet shall die."*
> *-Deuteronomy 18:20*

In this dispensation of the church, we are not messengers of God as were the Old Testament prophets. We will not be stoned to death if we get the message wrong. We are God's messengers of edification and building souls up. We are to build up the church with the gift of prophecy. We are required to test the spirits and develop certitude of the message we perceive. We must also have the character of Jesus Christ to deliver the word we perceive. In the New Testament we perceive, in the Old Testament the prophets received. Know the difference.

Prophetic Encouragement and Spiritual Alignment

The New Testament Gospels' type of prophetic ministry differs from Old Testament prophecy. In the New Testament, prophetic ministry— through the Holy Spirit—was poured out on all flesh (Acts 2:17). The Old Testament prophets received the word of God directly from the Holy Spirit while New Testament prophets perceive the word of God from the indwelling Holy Spirit. Why does the believer prophesy in the first place? "But one who prophesies speaks to men for edification and exhortation and consolation" (1 Corinthians 14:3).

God is love. He wants us to speak to His children in a kind way. God's greatest commandment is to love Him and no other gods. For us to have a relationship with God, we must dialogue with Him. He wants to edify us and encourage us. God wants exhortation. He wants the church to draw near to Him.

The reason God gave us the gift of prophecy was so we would encourage one another and add souls to the kingdom. Edification is building up and encouraging one another. "But encourage one another day after day, as long as it is still called 'Today,' so that none of you will be hardened by the deceitfulness of sin" (Hebrews 3:13). Here is where the prophetic ministry has its place in inner healing ministry: we are to strengthen the souls of the disciples so that they can love the Lord with all their hearts, all their minds, and all their strength! "Strengthening the souls of the disciples, encouraging them to continue in the faith, and saying, 'Through many tribulations we must enter the kingdom of God'" (Acts 14:22).

Hearing from God, we can use His words to spiritually realign a soul focused on the flesh and not on Jesus Christ.

> "Preach the word; be ready in season and out of season; reprove, rebuke, exhort, with great patience and instruction."
> -2 Timothy 4:2

How do we rebuke attitudes and behavior using prophetic gifts? God provides consolation to the afflicted and wounded souls. He comes alongside the afflicted souls to walk them out of their bondage and brokenness.

> "Blessed be the God and Father of our Lord Jesus Christ, the Father of mercies and God of all comfort, who comforts us in all our affliction so that we will be able to comfort those who are in any affliction with the comfort with which we ourselves are comforted by God"
> -2 Corinthians 1:3-4

Prophetic Ministry Etiquette

Prophetic ministry is instrumental in bringing inner healing. Prayer recipients seldom divulge everything sinful in their lifestyle. Many hide the sins they are truly shameful of, and it is that very sin that is causing their brokenness or affliction. God will reveal it and He will exercise the utmost compassion, grace, and mercy during the session. If you are new to this ministry, the prophetic will come to you over time, like a muscle reflex, as you use it. For the beginner, become a student of the story of the woman at the well (John 4) and study the compassion with which Jesus ministered. Closely guard your mouth, whether a beginner or a seasoned minister, and ask the Holy Spirit if what you're receiving is to be shared with the recipient or if it is tactical information. For instance, too many ministers tell an individual, "Oh, I see a demon on you!" when that isn't necessary information to share with the prayer recipient. In fact, if there are any mental issues, or if they are DID, they will never let go of that bad prophetic word. I tend to hold back on information I see spiritually in deliverance and DID prayer ministry sessions. Even though I have been doing this for some time, I will always quietly do checks and balances with the prayer ministers with me to discern if I am hearing correctly. If we all hear the same thing, then this becomes tactical information.

I don't always share what I am seeing. As an example of this in my ministry, I was working with a young woman who is a survivor of satanic ritual abuse. As I was praying with her, I saw a shadow figure walk through a closed door and stand next to my chair where I was sitting. I don't know if the shadow spirit knew I could see it. Under my breath, I bound witchcraft using my spiritual authority. The woman I was ministering to and the other counselor in the room couldn't hear me pray. As I prayed to bind the witchcraft from entering the room, the woman looked up at me and told me that the spirits were filling up the room. I didn't intend to be testing my spiritual discernment, but the teacher lent me a hand. The Holy Spirit let me see one of the manifestations so I could deal with it. The witchcraft and spiritual manifestations were shut down. It was tactical information and I used it to our advantage. The Holy Spirit did not release me into sharing with the others what was happening in the room. The occult spirits were in for a bit of a surprise.

If I do share prophetic tactical information, I do so in the form of a compassionate question. Show the person who came to you for help gentleness and respect. This approach is true, Holy Spirit-driven deliverance ministry. A questionable or immature minister would be an individual shouting out and binding all the demons they think they know, rather than allowing the Holy Spirit to drive the prayer session.

A Case of a Prophetic Minister with No Spiritual Direction

This incident I am about to share happened a few years ago. My wife, Lisa, and I were ministering at a corporate deliverance retreat that ministers to several hundred prayer recipients. This retreat started early in the morning, and Lisa and I had an hour-long drive to the location of the event. We got up early in the morning, and we were on-site at the retreat for the early pre-commencement intercession. The event was relatively big, with about fifty or so intercessors on hand for the prayer coverage. Lisa and I were assigned to a small group of intercessors to pray for each other and then go pray over the large auditorium before the retreat started. There were four intercessors assigned to our prayer team: Lisa, myself, an older gentleman, and a young lady in her mid-twenties named Julie. For our team's opening prayer, we started praying for one another, and Julie started receiving some prophetic words about the ministers on her team. Julie asked me if she could share with me what she was hearing from God. With intercessors, it's common to give prophetic words to one another during prayer. It's how we build each other up and prepare for battle. So for me, I was perfectly comfortable to hear what Julie was hearing from God. I gave Julie my permission to go ahead and tell me what she was hearing. Julie very calmly looked over at me and told me that she felt I wouldn't be effective in ministry today because I didn't spend time in the Word this morning. When I heard Julie's prophetic word, I looked at her puzzled. I was thinking, *"What kind of a prophetic word is that?"* I at first blamed my caffeine not working in my body and thought maybe I'd heard Julie wrong. Then Julie looked over at Lisa and told her she needed to call home because my middle son was in trouble right now and he needed her at home. By now Lisa and I were looking at each other kind of bewildered. Like, what on earth was that? Get behind us, Satan! The older gentleman with us had a smile on his face and said, "Isn't she pretty dead on? She has an amazing gift." Lisa and I looked at each other in complete disbelief. Julie's prophetic words were mortifying! Lisa and I were very proficient in our prophetic ministry by this time. We had led numerous prophetic outreaches into some dark territories. What came out of Julie's mouth was either soulish gibberish or purely demonic.

Julie wasn't demonized, but from her pride, she was operating out of deception. She was listening in on the wrong spiritual channel. She had little to no spiritual direction in her prophetic training. Without proper mentoring and correction, it is easy to fall into this trap. You tune into your soul, and from there the enemy can easily hijack your gift. Psychics and clairvoyants are using nothing more than a hijacked spiritual gift. Like Julie, nothing that comes out of your mouth will align with what God would want to tell his children. As for Julie's prophetic words for Lisa and I, these weren't prophetic words; they were demonic distractions. It was a no-brainer that I didn't spend time in the Word. I got up early for the long drive to the retreat where God wanted to set his people free. Julie's prophetic word for my wife was not from God at all. If it were an actual warning, we would have gotten a call from our middle son who would have told us something was wrong. There was no such confirmation to support Julie's bad prophecies. In fact, our middle son had a rather pleasant day that day. Nothing Julie had to share aligned with God. Julie's message was a demonic locution to throw us off our game for combat. Julie's church was ignorant of proper prophetic ministry and was holding her up on a pedestal. The truth of the matter is that people were getting hurt by her reckless prophetic ministry.

Under proper spiritual direction and mentoring, had Julie received a word like that, she would have processed it in her soul's intellect and unpacked it as an ungodly word. Then she would have said something along the lines of, "I think we should pray to cancel any assignments of the enemy and pray for protection over our families." Do you see the difference here? There is no element of distraction toward the ministers. And even if the enemy was or was not planning malice, the prayer team prays in unity for protection. The unity of the intercessory team now aligns more to what God would want a prophetic prayer ministry team to do. Prophetic words are questionable because man and his soul are fallible. A soul with proper spiritual direction and experience will know how to safely unpack a word, whether from God, the soul, or the enemy.

Remember, a prophetic word edifies the body of Christ and chases the heart of pre-believers. That is the key criterion for giving a prophetic word. As a prophetic minister, you must be equipped to operate in ministry and learn to discern what is from God and what isn't. Like our friend Julie, if she'd reached out to other ministers, she probably could have been better prepared for ministry. With proper direction in using her gift, Julie would have never given those negative prophetic words. My wife and I, and people I know who operate in prophetic ministry, have worked with more advanced ministers and have learned to take correction (i.e. spiritual direction). Getting equipped and participating at prophetic outreaches or with seasoned prophetic deliverance ministries is one of the many ways the Holy Spirit will raise you up in this. The other method is in your personal walk with the Holy Spirt.

Night Strike Ended through Hearing God

I would like to provide an example of how God instructs me and gives me direction in my ministry. In the summer of 2015, God told me through a series of dreams that I was to stop the Night Strike ministry in San Francisco and redeploy, alone, in San Francisco for a new ministry. As my ministry with trauma survivors increased, I started understanding dissociative identity disorder more. I was seeing a lot of homeless people who were both drug addicts and survivors of severe trauma, and they exhibited dissociative behaviors. In my spirit, I began to see that Night Strike ministry was not enough for what the homeless on the streets of San Francisco needed.

> "Indeed God speaks once, or twice, yet no one notices it. In a
> dream, a vision of the night, when sound sleep falls on men,
> while they slumber in their beds, then He opens the ears of men,
> and seals their instruction."
> -Job 33:14-15

The first in the series of dreams started with me in an old civic-looking building in San Francisco. I was talking to a member of my Night Strike team in the dream. My fellow minister looked me in the eyes and said, "I am in bondage to homosexuality and the occult, and until I deal with this, I will never be fully healed!"

I told him in the dream that I understood what he was going through and then he got up and left. A second later, another person came to sit down in front of me. He said, "I overheard what you said to that man. I, too, am in bondage to homosexuality and the occult. Can you help me?" I knew from inside this prophetic dream what God was telling me. After spending nearly a decade in street ministry in San Francisco, I was well-versed with the demonic powers in the city. San Francisco has multiple high-level spirits. There is a spirit of mind control from the 1960s (LSD, Haight-Ashbury, Charles Manson, Jim Jones, The People's Temple). There is a spirit of perversion (Mitchell Bros pornography in the '70s, homosexuality, and S &M) throughout the city. A powerful political spirit directs the nation from rulings in the Ninth Circuit Court, and a powerful occult spirit is also present (Anton LaVey, modern day Satanism, Chi, Yoga, and Sexual Yoga).

Through this series of dreams, I knew I was to start a new inner healing ministry to help the traumatized and bring an end to Night Strike.

Then I had another dream. I was driving a big rig truck, and it prophetically represented Night Strike ministry. I was on a freeway and the big rig ran out of gas, and I had to get out of the truck and walk. I walked a good mile with my gas can to a freeway exit with gas stations. I remember in the dream going from gas station to gas station at this location, and not one station sold diesel fuel for my truck. The truck, the dream metaphor for Night Strike, had run out of fuel. That dream weighed on my heart. You know God's voice, and I knew what he'd just told me in the dream: that Night Strike had come to an end even though it was still operating full force on Friday nights. My heart sank with that dream.

Not even a week after I had that dream, a friend of mine, Gina, called me and told me that she had two prophetic ministers doing a house meeting. She knew I was busy on Fridays, but wondered if we could all meet for lunch on Saturday. We didn't know what to expect at the meeting other than to connect. We didn't come seeking a prophetic word. We were looking for connections for our prophetic evangelism ministry outreaches. We talked about what the two ministers were doing while visiting house churches across the northwest. It was probably towards the end of the lunch when one minister, Bill, looked at me straight in the eye and told me he had a word for me. Because I am a deliverance minister, my natural inclination is always that of a generous and polite skeptic, so I listened to what Bill had to say. Bill told me that I was in charge of a very large ministry which was coming to an end. God had ordained it. He said, "You have taken the torch of someone else and you honored the ministry which was given to you. But you know full well God has given you no successors to pass the torch on to, and God is shutting down the ministry. God wants you to do this in a timely manner in order to catch the next wave of the Holy Spirit."

At that moment, I was in tears. Bill had delivered the context of the big rig dream I had about Night Strike a few nights earlier. Night Strike had come to an end, and I felt in the spirit I had to do it in a month—before Lisa and I left for prophetic evangelism ministry at Burning Man (in August of 2015).

Many of my close team members and spiritual confidantes knew I'd heard clearly from God. They understood my obedience in following God on this new endeavor. However, since I had taken over Night Strike from a well-known minister, and run it for the past eight years, many of the minister's followers didn't believe I had correctly heard from God to shut down this ministry. I honored the ministry founders with a phone call and told them what God had instructed me to do, and they blessed my act of obedience to God. It was other people who were fickle. Many people didn't want me to end Night Strike, and I lost 90 percent of ministry funding. Funding didn't matter to me, well . . . actually it did. I lost all the funding for my future outreaches in 2016. But I knew God was doing a corporate reorganization in my ministry and the most important thing was to follow his direction. The new ministry in the city of San Francisco has launched, and so far, we have one survivor of severe trauma free from his crystal meth drug addiction. 2016 has been a building year for this new ministry. It is still not funded in any way, but the inner healing miracles have been priceless. When I was told to end Night Strike, God spoke to the heart of a friend of mine, Matthew Klosterman, whose mother, was actually the lead intercessor for Night Strike, several years prior, to take to the streets in ministry. Matt didn't know I was leaving the streets, but God instructed Matt to pick up the homeless ministry as I was being redirected to another campaign in the battle for San Francisco's revival.

I presented this situation here to illustrate that a real prophetic word can be ground shaking, and God will use it to separate the tares from the wheat to accomplish His will. Real prophecy from God moves in power. I have no regrets for being obedient, and I know I caught the wave of the Holy Spirit for my new ministry.

God may speak to you thorugh amazing spiritual dreams. Dreams are a powerful form of prophetic ministry. God raised me up in deliverance ministry through dreams when I was in a church that had no clue what deliverance ministry was. Quite frankly, when I first heard the word deliverance, back in 2007, I thought it was about an old Burt Reynolds's movie named Deliverance.

Hearing God through Discursive Meditation

As a simple exercise to learn how you hear from God (whether through seeing, hearing, knowing, or sensing), sit in a chair and just relax and meditate on the words of Psalm 46.

> "Be still and know that I am God, and I will be exalted above, I will be exalted in the earth."
> -Psalm 46:10 KJV

See what the Holy Spirit reveals to you during this time of meditation on the Word. Biblical meditation means you are reading the Word of God and letting your soul process it. Meditating on the words you read in the Bible is called *discursive meditation*. As you read the same verse over, like Psalm 46, you pause and listen and see if God is going to speak to you on this text of Scripture. Discursive meditation is not Zen meditation! You are not purging yourself, rather you are filling yourself with God's Word and the Holy Spirit. A big difference! Use contemplation. Allow your soul's imagination and intellect to wonder as God gives you revelation.

Teaching Soul's to Hear for Themselves

In the Western church, we have become lazy in our spiritual walk. We outsource everything spiritual we should be doing ourselves. We have far too many souls that can't connect with God. I have found that the obsessive seeking of prophetic words at conferences is a telltale sign of souls that can't connect with God. They pray for an impartation of hearing God at the conference, get caught up in the spiritual whirlwind of the events, and go home still unable to connect with God. There's a reason Jesus told his disciples to go to their quiet place and pray (Matthew 6). Jesus was outlining to his disciples how to connect with God. Connecting with God builds the relationship with Him. Don't expect supernatural experiences to be your benchmark. Jesus just wants to be with you. He's more about the intimacy than about the experiences. When you're in the right place in your relationship with Him, He will teach you how to hear Him. And like I shared here, God may speak to you in dreams. Not every dream is a spiritual dream. We must discern and weigh what is supernatural and what is natural whenever we work with God. Hearing from God requires prayer discipline and time well spent with the indwelling Jesus.

CHAPTER 8

Soul Wounds and Soul Fracturing

A soul wound is a deep emotional inner pain that resides in the heart and soul. We tend to carry our soul wounds from an experience from our childhood. A parent repeatedly telling his child he was an unwanted baby is a common form of emotional abuse that creates a soul wound in the heart. Another common soul wound is a father calling his daughter fat or stupid. The child growing up in an emotionally and verbally abusive environment will create a soul wound. If the emotional abuse is severe enough, it may even fracture the child's soul into multiple identities. Sometimes reinforcement of a soul wound may come from a parent showing favoritism to another sibling. Unhealthy childhood attachment issues exist between the parents and the child. As an adult, the heart and soul may relive these emotions and inner pains when memories, or similar situational feelings, are triggered. Not all soul wounds originate from childhood. A wife catching her husband having an extramarital affair will no doubt create a soul wound of rejection, anger, betrayal of trust, resentment, bitterness, and unforgiveness.

Soul wounds come into play in deliverance ministry because demons know these wounds harbor unforgiveness. As an example, demons may have no legal rights to a soul but won't leave when you expel them. A demon with no legal rights will attach itself to the stronghold of a soul wound. The demon will not leave until the issue with the soul wound has been resolved and healed.

Soul Wounds and Inner Healing

Many deliverance ministers feel the emotions to the soul wound can be released through a forgiveness prayer. If the trauma that caused the soul wound is mild, this may work. However, most soul wounds are very deep and come from severe emotional, physical, and sexual abuse. Depending on the severity of the soul wound, it may take more time to deal with the forgiveness than you have allotted for the prayer ministry session. Some soul wounds may require years to heal through Christian counseling with someone who understands trauma and inner healing. Counseling sessions may be required to determine that the individual is dealing with a soul wound and not a dissociated, fractured soul. A mocking spirit can also be a fractured part of the soul that is angry at God. Angry parts love to be confrontational with deliverance ministers.

Soul wounds manifest from a personal violation, broken trust, rejection, abuse, unhealed emotions, and painful memories. Because of the severity of the wound, prayer ministry must be used for inner healing to walk the recipient through the healing process with Jesus. A soul wound is a stronghold. Because of the severity of the unhealed emotions, the soul can't move past the memories and move on to forgiveness and healing. Jesus came to heal the brokenhearted and set the captives free.

Soul wounds surface quite often in deliverance ministry sessions. In fact the night before I wrote this chapter, I was conducting a deliverance prayer session with one of my ministry friends, Adrienne. I called in Adrienne for backup on this session since I was working with a woman, Jenny, who was coming out of the occult. She went through some hard times in her life, and during a weak point in her life, she decided to take up divination through angels—a form of tarot card reading that communicates to false angels of light. There was a lot of Christian-ese in this New Age occult practice, and it could suck in any Christian unaware of the deception involved. Jenny said she would have visitations from false archangels and they would tell her things. It wasn't long before the false archangels started showing up constantly, as well as bringing what looked like her dead relatives. Things got out of hand. The spirits started tormenting her and showing up all the time. Jenny tried rejecting the demons so they would leave. The demons started perpetrating her body with pain, especially in the spiritually sensitive areas of the hands—which held the tarot cards, and her ears—which she used to hear the locutions of the demonic.

When Adrienne and I ministered with Jenny in the counseling office, we were able to shut down, through prayer, some of the demonic activity. There was a false trinity and a false angelic choir at play. What is interesting about this is that most times you encounter a false trinity and false angels of light, it is with cases of Satanism. In this case, it was an angel tarot card reader. These were low-level demons masquerading as satanic level angelic beings. To expel the spirits, Jenny had to renounce her tarot card and occult practices. However, one little pesky evil spirit wouldn't leave, and this wasn't a mocking spirit. We took a break from the deliverance session and just asked God for revelation about the spirit. A few minutes into prayer, a mutual word of wisdom came into the ministry team that this was a generational spirit from her mother. We resumed prayer and ministry and found out that one of the occult spirits was clinging to a generational soul wound of rejection. There was a generational curse of unwanted babies in Jenny's family line. Jenny's mom told her that she didn't want Jenny when she was born. The Holy Spirit gave us the revelation about a deep soul wound Jenny was quietly harboring. Jenny started weeping as the Holy Spirit manifested around her for healing. The direction of the battle then shifted to an inner healing of the soul wound of rejection. There was still a long, drawn-out battle over a period of months with Jenny. The revelation of the soul wound was pivotal in the warfare.

In prayer sessions, when a soul wound gets healed, we have witnessed Jesus bring a very gentle form of deliverance. If a demon is present, the indwelling and incarnate Jesus expels it. The Holy Spirit heals the wound through tears. The crying is a manifestation of the Holy Spirit impacting

the soul and heart. You can have many tear-filled sessions of inner healing before the final liberation. It's all in God's timing.

> *"He makes me lie down in green pastures; He leads me beside*
> *quiet waters. He restores my soul; He guides me in the paths of*
> *righteousness for His name's sake."*
> *-Psalm 23:2-3*

Ministry for soul wounds centers around Jesus resolving the conflicts
of the diseased attitudes from the ungodly belief system. The ungodly
belief system is composed of interwoven lies to reinforce the sense of
hopelessness. From this the diseased attitudes about oneself take shape.
Diseased attitudes include self-imposed metrics of never being able to
measure up, perfectionism, bitterness, anger, blame, unforgiveness, failure, shame, and rejection, to name a few.

Super Strongholds and Dissociative Identity Disorder

As I present Dissociative Identity Disorder (DID), keep in mind that it is
a ministry that requires expertise in the field. Healing souls with severe
trauma requires an established team and community. Dissociative Identity
Disorder (DID) is the fracturing of the human soul into multiple parts
through severe traumatic experiences from childhood. This fracturing
or dissociation is by God's design to protect the fragile mind of a child
from severe traumatic experiences. Dissociation allows the child's brain
to emotionally and psychologically detach from a hopeless situation of
severe abuse, trauma, and pain. The memories and emotions of the horrific event become disconnected from the normal function of the soul's
faculties. This mental disconnect allows the primary faculties of the soul
to go on functioning as if the trauma never occurred.

It is a God created design of the child's mind to disconnect from
severe trauma and reconnect when the danger is over. It's a component
of the fight-or-flight response. When the child is repeatedly under traumatic experiences such as emotional, physical, sexual, or ritual abuse,
the dissociation becomes reflexive and immediately takes the child out
of trauma. After that the dissociation can be triggered by trauma, anxi-
ety, or feeling threatened. Toni Taigen, founder of In the Potter's Hands

counseling and prayer ministry, has defined *triggering* as the follwing emotional response,

> When I feel an extreme emotion about something that just happens or happened recently. Like when someone makes a joke that shouldn't be a big deal but totally throws you off for the rest of the day. Or someone expresses disapproval of you, or you think that someone looked at you funny. Suddenly, you find yourself feeling off and your parts are going crazy and maybe you're feeling anxiety shame guilt depression etc. A trigger is a wound I have that is not healed. A lie that I believe about myself.

The dissociation becomes a defensive mechanism and can surface at any time, depending on how it is triggered. For survivors of severe childhood trauma, multiple identities may develop within the soul from unhealthy and exhaustive or deliberately invoked (ritual abuse) dissociation from trauma. These multiple identities are what I refer to as *soul fractures* or *parts*. The multiple identities are states of consciousness that can carry out various roles or jobs for individuals who have fractured souls. When an identity surfaces and the state of consciousness changes from one part or identity to another, this brain activity is called *switching*.

A survivor of severe childhood trauma may have multiple identities, perhaps hundreds or even thousands, depending on what happened to him. This collection of multiple identities in a soul is called a *system of dissociative parts*, or simply called a *system*. A DID system is a super stronghold. Multiple identities are in bondage to a demonically orchestrated web of lies of ungodly beliefs. Fear and the reliving of pain are methods used to keep identities imprisoned in the soul. The DID stronghold also uses attachment issues, where the mind is led to believe that it is incapable of building lasting relationships with others.

Cases involving DID can be a bit tricky since they are not healings that can come through conventional deliverance ministry. Many times, people already know they're DID because they have a committee of internal voices or thoughts inside their heads that carry out nonstop chatter. Because a lot of information isn't mainstream on DID, most Christians have mistaken these fractured human parts to be demons. In some cases, demons are present, but the deliverance won't be useful because angry human parts may want the demons there with them.

Many church pastors and deliverance ministers have been fooled by parts portraying themselves as demons and tried to cast them out as mocking spirits. These are mocking human parts. Do not associate a mocking spirit all the time with a mocking part. You must be aware that angry human parts mock and look like evil spirits. I don't believe in mocking spirits; the spirits only mock you when they know they've got you cornered and you're using human reasoning against them. When the mocking part may arise, start asking the prayer recipient if he experienced any trauma as a child. DID surfaces in children who were trafficked, abused by parents, or ritually abused, all before the age of eight. The most severe fracturing of the soul occurs before the age of four in an abusive environment.

Soul Wounds and Soul Fracturing Discernment

A soul wound is an emotional wound of the heart that is strictly and deeply emotional and severe, but it doesn't involve dissociation. A fractured soul is a soul with wounds that may have splintered into multiple identities. A soul wound may be an indicator of a fractured soul, but it takes someone with proper training and experience to discern this. The rule of thumb is not to pursue Sozo or deliverance ministry on these individuals who may be severe trauma survivors. Soul wounds can heal over weeks to months or even years. Soul fracturing may take years of consistent ministry, on a weekly basis, to bring inner healing to the fractured parts. There are currently not a lot of ministries out there that work with DID and focus on it. Currently, M16 Ministries works in conjunction with In the Potter's Hands counseling, here in Northern California. There is also CARE in Michigan and Restoration in Christ Ministries in Virginia. These are the ministries that work with the tough dissociation cases from severe trauma. When you come across this, you need to get mentored and educated by ministries that operate and equip in these areas, because you will be working with severe trauma and horrific incidents that were part of the fracturing of the soul. This is especially true with ritual abuse cases. Not all people are cut out for this ministry. It is very graphic and you must be steadfast and able to help in very dark ministry sessions. This steadfast posture only comes from the Holy Spirit.

CHAPTER 9

Ritual Abuse Survivors

Ritual abuse survivor ministry is a category of spiritual warfare all unto itself. It's not deliverance minsitry, and it's not exorcism. These cases walk on the fringe of the deepest darkest horrors, as well as conspiracy theories. Ritual abuse is extremely difficult to prove, but its crime scene fingerprints are left behind in the people who survived it as children. These cases are challenging and are difficult to wrap your mind around and comprehend. You will work with people who went through horrific childhoods and had their souls deliberately fractured for the purpose of participating in secret society rituals. I seldom share information of what I know with clients because I want to hear their story uncoerced. Over the past years, what I have heard is the same types of stories unfold, and that secret society dark magic ritual abuse and mind control programming is real. The people I have had the opportunity to work with in their inner healing are some of the most spiritual, prayer-minded, Jesus-loving Christians one can ever meet. They're in a fight for inner healing that takes years or even decades. Their pursuit and passion for Christ are relentless as they work through the trauma they endured from their childhood life.

The stereotypical view of satanic ritual abuse (SRA) from the Christian perspective is that of a woman who escaped from a coven and is a bride of Satan. Christians always get excited thinking they saved the bride of Satan. Every book you read by Christians who saved a person from

93

SRA always flaunt they rescued the bride of Satan. Keep in mind, everything about satanic rituals is a mockery of Jesus Christ. Every Christian is the bride of Jesus, the mystical body of Christ. The church is the bride of Jesus. If Jesus has His bride, then Satan mimics that with his brides. A fairly recent charismatic movie featured a deliverance minister that rescued an SRA survivor. Of course, the number one thing the testimony in the movie focused on was that she was a bride of Satan. The story focused on her rescue being timely because they got her before being forced to marry Satan. There were a lot of things presented in this movie that were so wrong, so I want to give you a clearer picture here of what SRA is and why deliverance ministry is not something you should do on these survivors. Ritual abuse survivors require a different approach to ministry for their inner healing.

Types of Ritual Abuse

Ritual abuse is not limited to Satanism. There are several forms of ritual abuse, the common categories being satanic, occult, and secret society ritual abuse, Christian cult ritual abuse, sex trafficking, and alien abductees (which is SRA in disguise). Whatever the category, all the ritual abuse involves the deliberate splintering of a child's consciousness through severe trauma and pain. The purpose of the fracturing of the human consciousness, the soul, is purely for two purposes: mind control for participation in dark society rituals, and for summoning dark power from demons. Hundreds to thousands of parts may be created in a child's consciousness solely for the role of participating in specific types of rituals. In my work, I have come across ritual abuse with the following secret societies which involve the occult. These include Satanism, Luciferianism, Illuminati, Freemasons, Odd Fellows, and the Rosicrucians. The Internet is flourishing with disinformation on these secret societies. Good luck in finding any useful information nailing down their occult activity. I don't waste my time researching secret societies. Each path of investigation is a splinter down deliberately misleading rabbit holes that go nowhere. Besides, information on what these secret societies did using the occult have no value in helping these souls receive inner healing. Instead, I focus all my attention on Jesus Christ and how his compassion and ministry will heal these fractured souls. The way to heal these souls is to focus on how Jesus operates in these ministry sessions.

Ritual Abuse Perpetrators

Early on in my ministry with ritual abuse survivors, I wanted to know what kind of monsters could do this to a child. As I worked more with survivors, one horrific fact bubbled to the surface. Ritual abuse is generational, and it's incestual in nature. The monsters who did this were the victim's own mothers and fathers, who themselves were programmed and fractured by their parents. Satan builds his church through generational slavery and bondage. The salvation of Jesus Christ brings love, inner peace, and hope to the soul. Satan is out to destroy everything Jesus Christ represents. In Satanism, there is hatred of the family unit, no free will, slavery, bondage, violence, incest, mind control, and lies upon lies. Families can't leave the coven because of the threat of killing individuals, their children, or their entire family. On top of that, their minds are so splintered and programmed, it is extremely difficult for them to leave the coven.

Mind control programming and ritual abuse start in what should otherwise be the sanctity of the mother's womb. It's not uncommon for the programming to take place before birth. In generational Satanism, by the time the child is eight years old, a majority of the ritual parts have already been created. Not all programming is generational. I have several cases where the next-door neighbors were trusted family friends and closet Satanists. The neighbors had trusted access to the children. After all, how could your nice neighbors be Satanists? These Satanists prey upon children who are very young, usually of the age of three to four years old, and program them for Satanism. Through programming, the children were threatened never to tell their parents about what was happening to them. Trauma and violence occur to the children in ways that don't leave marks on the body, such as drowning and electrocution, just to name a few. The trauma is sufficient to cause the child to dissociate, and the energy of the pain is enough to attract demons. Yes, severe trauma from children attracts demons. It's like chumming the water.

Programming and Double Binds

Jesus is actively chasing each and every one of us. He wants us to surrender to Him with all our heart, all our mind, all our strength. Satan doesn't want us to have any free will. He is all about slavery. No one will ever surrender to Satan with all his heart, will, and strength, and he knows it. Satan is pure evil, and he hates the human race. Those who seek Satan do so under their own fallen nature of being deceived into acquiring special power and knowledge. Ritual abuse is different and it doesn't involve curses from dabbling in the occult. In incestual (generational) Satanism, programming is used to break the will of the souls of children.

In ways which I don't completely understand, nor care to understand, the fetus is mentally traumatized through rituals. The goal of this programming ritual is to split the baby's soul in two. This fracturing is called *twinning of identities*, where one fractured part of the soul will become the day host and the other will be the night host as the child grows up. During the ritual, the fetus undergoes extreme trauma, to the point of near death or even death. The child's trauma generates energy for the demonic spirits to enter the fractured soul. You get the idea; this is evil beyond our comprehension.

Duplicitous Programming

The *night host* identity is primarily responsible for the programmed identities that will participate in the night rituals. At midnight, or sometimes as early as sundown, the night host will wake up and start triggering the parts for the late-night rituals.

During the day, the *day host* covers for all the ritual abuse that goes on at night. The day host parts are rarely or ever aware of their night host parts. The day host is responsible for the child to live out his cover story for what is going on. With generational Satanism, the family may even go to church on Sunday, because their day hosts are programmed to attend. This double nature is called *duplicity programming*. Duplicity programming will also interfere with the Christian host when he tries to spiritually connect with God or read his Bible. A duplicitous programmed identity will surface and insanely rattle blasphemous thoughts or interfere with the reading comprehension during the Bible study session.

As I mentioned previously, a family programmed in generational Satanism will attend church on Sunday, yet the night prior they will be doing rituals and sacrifices for a successful harvest. This split personality spirituality is duplicity programming. Duplicity shows up consistently during prayer ministry. You will be working with evangelizing an identity to meet the true Jesus Christ. [Keep in mind: in this ministry we make a distinction between the true Jesus and the false Jesus used in ritual programming.] Then, in a flash of thought, the same part will become blasphemous and hate Jesus. Duplicity programming makes it difficult for the fractured parts to seek the help of the true Jesus. Duplicitous parts get activated by trigger words using the name of Jesus and the Trinity. It's common for the duplicitous part to believe it is a demon. When a deliverance minister encounters this duplicitous part, he will be deceived into believing it is a mocking spirit.

Duplicity programming keeps the lie of the generational Satanism hidden from the outside world. Duplicity also plays a role in causing chaos in the identity when it tries to surrender to the true Jesus. Healing identities from duplicity require a lot of patience and may take a single session to possibly years of prayer ministry to resolve the double bind. The overall goal of the double binds and duplicity are to keep the fractured parts in a traumatic state of hopelessness.

Double-Bind Programming

Double binds prevent the fractured soul from stepping out of bondage. A *double bind* is a programming mechanism used by the occult which conditions the fractured parts of the soul into believing there is no hope whatsoever of ever being set free from this nightmare. Early double bind conditioning involves the occult taking a child, about four or five years old, and forcing him to choose between the lives of one of two pets. One pet must die, and if the child doesn't choose a pet, the occult programmer will kill both pets and blame the child for his lack of obedience in choosing one pet. Part of the reasoning behind the double bind is to teach the child that he is evil. Next time the child chooses a pet to spare, the programmer will reinforce the programming with the lie that a pet had to die because the child was evil. The traumatic programming intensifies as the child gets a little bit older. The occult will introduce a false Jesus into the rituals. The presence of false Jesus will reinforce the occult lie that Jesus can never help the child. When the child is in trauma, the occult programmer will tell the child to call out to Jesus for help. When the child does call out to false Jesus, the programmer will, as an example, punch the child in the face. This horrific conditioning goes on until the child's will completely breaks and the double bind of calling out to false Jesus is mentally reinforced with pain. Again, false Jesus participated in horrific and disgusting rituals with the child. This programming plays back and the child gets beaten up internally, in the soul, when he considers calling out to Jesus for help. The system has no concept of who the true Jesus is and no interest in contacting Him for help. This programming gets triggered during prayer ministry, and we work with the true Jesus Christ to resolve the lie of the double bind. Programming is supernatural and involves demonic spirits interlaced in the programming somewhere. The programming keeps the fractured identity a slave to Satan, keeps the lies of Satanism reinforced in the system, and prevents the occult identity from getting evangelized, which supernaturally heals the identity.

Ritual Abuse Parts

A ritual abuse system can have thousands of parts in the system, and each part carries out a specific function. I can write volumes on the parts present in a system, but I am going to focus on a few here. Let's start with the original soul that was fractured. One of the key parts of the system is the core identity, which is the soul Jesus formed in the womb.[1] The core identity is a remaining fragment of the original soul before the programming occurred. A core identity is rarely present when ministering to survivors. With ritual abuse, many times the core identity is locked away somewhere in the soul and tormented, or it is in a suspended state. When

---

1 Psalm 139:13

you minister with a Christian that is a ritual abuse survivor, you will be working 90 percent of the time with the Christian host. A therapist may call this a primary presenter, but in ritual abuse ministry, this is the Christian host. The Christian host is present most of the time during his daily life routines and the ministry sessions. The Christian host is responsible for the daily sanctification of the healed and unhealed soul. Healing comes to the soul through the faith and the perseverance of the Christian host. The Christian host is responsible for evangelizing the other identities in the system. The deeper the spiritual life the Christian host has with the true Jesus, the deeper the healing moves into the system. During healing, the Christian host may go away under the guidance and healing of the Holy Spirit to allow another part to assume the presenter role in order to resolve his double bind. This part switching may occur for a day, a couple of days, weeks, or even months. The important thing to do is to follow what Jesus is doing in these healings. Both the Christian host and the ministry team must be very patient in what Jesus is doing when He heals parts. During this time, we know from ministry experience that the Christian host doesn't entirely go away, he is present and doing his job as the system evangelist for Jesus. The Christian host is not reachable by the part, but he can feel the Christian host's presence.

When Jesus resolves the double bind with the part or parts and the part chooses to surrender to Jesus, he receives healing. The Christian host will then switch back in as the presenter and resume the daily life living and spiritual faith role. A strong Christian host is vital to inner healing. Occult parts will want to control the healing ministry session. The Christian host doesn't try to control the healing with the ministry session; the Christian host surrenders to the indwelling incarnate true Jesus. Because you are working with Christian parts that are anywhere from three to sixteen years old, you must be very vigilant in your spiritual direction. I have worked with a six-year-old Christian host presenter in a sixty-year-old body, who was capable of memorizing nearly all the verses in Scripture. The child part, the Christian host, was never taught how to connect with the indwelling God. The six-year-old part was a charismatic Christian and surmised that to experience God, he needed to mimic what he saw other charismatic Christians do in church. After observing this individual, Jesus revealed to me that this Christian presenter was believing his deep self-fabricated spiritual encounter acts because that's what he watched other Charismatics do. The Charismatics appear to experience intense open visions and powerful physical manifestations of the Holy Spirit.

I come from a charismatic background, so I am not putting these people down. I have a strange combination of holding a degree in computational physics as well as being a charismatic Christian. That puts me radically in the middle. My science/engineering/charismatic spiritual background allows me to quickly identify those who present themselves as having faux spiritual experiences. And there are a lot who do put on quite a show. Sadly, other eyes are observing them and think that is what an experience with God is. When it came time to work with this six-year-old Christian host, it was hard to teach this little soul to pray and have sublime encounters with the indwelling Jesus. Mental prayer is 98 percent uneventful. It's simply dialogue with the true Jesus Christ. The six-year-old thought every prayer experience was to be a supernatural encounter with visions and angels. Spiritual direction is everything in this ministry when working with the Christian host. I have had some Christian hosts who were teens in forty and fifty-year-old bodies. The teen Christian presenters were able to develop a deep interior prayer life. They also experienced gentle encounters with true Jesus, and He would come to their aid when the system was becoming chaotic. I have also worked with teen Christian hosts that were under siege from duplicitous parts and were being constantly shut down in their mental prayer. You must work with each Christian host where he is at in life and in his healing. If it takes a week or several years to work with a Christian host so he can pray, then that is what it takes. There is no timeframe around all of this. Some may take months to years!

A control part is just as its name implies. Many times before a Christian host is strong enough to assume control as a primary presenter, there will be a control part that operates and hides behind a primary presenter. The control parts seldom reveal themselves unless they want to surrender to Jesus, but you might know what the part acts like when it switches in. Many times the control part takes on a messiah role in the system.

There can be thousands of identities in a system. Don't be surprised if you encounter parts of the opposite sex. There are also perpetrating parts all over the ritual abuse system. These are identities trained to keep the ritual parts in their programming roles and relive the trauma. For instance, one child part may come up in a session and divulge a secret about a ritual, then a second later he is screaming in agony. This invoking of pain is from a perpetrating part which was triggered to inflict pain on the part you are working with in the session. He may scream with sudden back pain, stabbing, or act like he's being drowned, choked, or electrocuted. These are the actions of a perpetrating part, and many times these parts are wrongly discerned to be demons by deliverance ministers. If you have no spiritual discernment in this ministry, remember, thousands of little parts are studying you and learning ways to control you. Avoid deliverance ministry during these sessions, even if the Christian host asks you for deliverance. Yes, there are demons present, but another human part is playing games with you. The part that made the pact with the demon is trying to pick a fight with you, knowing full well the demon won't leave. This situation doesn't mean you can't take authority over the demon. Bind the demon and order it to leave the session so that you can evangelize the human part.

In the authority of Jesus Christ I separate the human part from the demonic.

The demon is present through the violations inflicted upon the body through trauma and pain. The demon doesn't have legal rights through sin. The demon is present because the human part has been deceived into believing the spirit is his protector. When the part surrenders to Jesus, the demon is evicted as a part of the healing from Jesus.

You will also encounter old people parts in a system, which were created when the child was, for example, only four years old. These parts can be programming images of the parents, grandparents, or other occult people who were involved in the ritual mind control programming. The programmer image is heavily protected with duplicitous programming to keep the minister away from these parts.

Dealing with the Occult

It takes a special prayer team that God organizes to minister to the survivors of occult rituals. You never take this on alone. A deliverance prayer team is not equipped to handle this level of warfare. It attacks individuals, families, businesses, marriages, and finances. You must understand the difference between a battle in your dominion and fighting in the heavenly realms. Learn how to operate in these theaters of battle. The safest way to learn about this is to get mentored. Pray and ask the Holy Spirit if you belong in this fight. There is a huge chasm between wanting to learn how to help these people and being brought into the fight by the Holy Spirit. Let the Holy Spirit release you into this ministry. If your home is dysfunctional, work on healing your home environment first, then pursue this. The demons will exploit a dysfunctional environment and ruthlessly destroy your home to keep you out of the fight. The people I work with and I are in solid marriages, or solid singles in their faith, and we have seen some crazy ways the demonic tries to stir up things in our marriages and our lives. If you're dealing with any sin in your life, work on that sanctification first and build up your faith. How do you know when you're ready for this? The Holy Spirit will bring it to your doorstep. That's how He works. I had people brought to me when I didn't know the first thing about SRA. I never sought out any of these ministries of deliverance, ritual abuse, or exorcism. The Holy Spirit gradually brought the ministry to me. This process the Holy Spirit uses in equipping us I refer to as *seasons* in ministry training. That's how he prepares you for battles in the occult and working with occult survivors.

Prayer Ministry

Jesus heals the parts. Therapists call this *integration*. As a word to the wise, never use the word integration to an unhealed part because the word the part(s) heard was disintegration. As in being vaporized or destroyed. If a part doesn't want to receive healing in the moment, don't push it. Get to know the part and listen to what the part tells you. It may reveal the double bind as to why the part won't talk with the true Jesus.

Open the prayer session with the Christian host praying to establish the true Jesus Christ for the ministry prayer session.

> *True Jesus, Son of God, who came to earth, over two thousand years ago through virgin birth, lived on earth as God incarnate, led a sinless holy life, was the only true blood atonement for our sins, died on the cross, and rose again in three days. It is you I address when I call out to you. I bind all evil spiritual representations of you. I ask you to shut down all false representations of you in my system.*

> *I ask this your name, true Jesus. Amen.*

After establishing the true Jesus, ask the true Jesus to take you to the parts He wants to work with today. Do not call up parts. Work with the parts that show up to the session. There is no methodology to this ministry session, only the absolute compassion of Jesus Christ. These parts aren't evil, they are the remnants of violated children that need His healing. Demons pop up in sessions, and so do occult loyal parts that will try to use witchcraft on you. Just deal with the distraction that is before you, bind it, and then resume ministry.

Conclusion

The people I work with who are survivors, I also call my friends. I never cease to be amazed at their depth of faith and love for Jesus Christ. Horrible things happened to them as children. Many were robbed of a healthy family life because the devil chose to be a destroyer of their family line, but their souls are relentless in chasing Jesus for their freedom. In these sessions, I have had the privilege to witness miracles of inner healing on a daily basis. Again, the mystical encounters that occur are sublime as Jesus heals the brokenhearted and sets the captive parts free.

CHAPTER 10

Prophetic Ministry with Fractured Souls

I n my early days of deliverance ministry, I learned that the most powerful inner healing sessions included prophetic words of knowledge. When I started working with survivors of severe trauma, I found the worst thing I could do to these souls was use prophetic ministry. Keep in mind that I am a prophetic minister, both in warfare sessions and outreaches. I operate in the prophetic. I don't want you to think I am against the prophetic ministry here. This book has advanced topics, so I would like to present some concerns and some red flags every minister needs to be aware of in this ministry. If you are ministering to an individual whom you believe to be DID or bipolar, I strongly advise against sharing what you see or hear in the prophetic realm with these afflicted souls. Because we are dealing with multiple identities, some parts (identities) love Jesus and some hate Jesus. The prophetic ministry provides for the inner perfect storm of the soul when there is a confrontation between parts for Jesus and angry parts of the fractured soul against Jesus.

The perfect storm typically occurs when the prayer minister tells the recipient that Jesus is going to heal all the fractured parts miraculously. Although this is biblically sound, it is still a soulish prophetic word. God doesn't heal the fractured soul instantaneously because this would violate the free will of each part in the fractured soul. For example, adults survivors, who in their childhood, were traumatized in child pornography rings or trafficked, or ritually abused, could have tens, hundreds, or even thousands of identities in the fractured soul system. When God chases the non-fractured, whole souls, to follow Him as their lord and savior, He does so by addressing the individual's brokenness. Through resolution and healing, the soul discovers the compassion of Jesus Christ. The same is true when He works with all the parts in a fractured soul. He woes each one to follow Him.

Jesus is chasing our heart in its brokenness, which is how most of us accept Him as our savior. Jesus extends this respect of free will to the fractured splinters of the soul so they may seek Him and be healed. It may seem like it would take a long time to heal thousands of identities, but just remember that Jesus is omnipresent. If there are a few thousand identities, Jesus can minister to all of them. However, we should never prophetically tell a person with DID that God is going to heal him all at once. To the thousands of parts, they hear that God is going to obliterate them and that the only surviving part will be the Christian host. The parts will obsess over this and even shut down their ministry time with Jesus, thinking He is going to disintegrate them at the time of healing. The clinical word "integration" is not very representative of what happens when parts heal. The identities perceive integration as a complete removal of their existence. Parts not ready for healing do not want to hear about a miraculous healing from Jesus for this very reason. Jesus will evangelize the parts first and then build up their trust in Him. When the parts are ready, Jesus will walk them through their healing. For this reason, when a minister gives a prophetic word of a miraculous healing of parts, the word may not have come from Jesus, but from the minister's soul.

Prayer ministry to DID souls is a ministry that requires mentoring and training. While the rule of ministry is to abstain from giving the DID prayer recipients prophetic words, I have a few survivors I work with that I do give prophetic words to because they are far enough along in their healing. And with these prophetic words, I keep it to words of encouragement. In prophetic ministry, never write a check you can't cash.

Too many ministers do this. Soul-based prophetic ministry does more damage than good, which means these words aren't from God. Again, prophetic ministry during these sessions is mostly for tactical purposes. Whatever I hear from God, I keep God's strategies to myself as to where He wants me to be in these spiritual battles and healings. The information is for partnering with what Jesus is doing in the healing of the fractured soul. Be aware that with ritual abuse survivors, they have duplicitous church parts that listen for prophetic words and are programmed to derail the prayer session when you use it openly.

Prophetic words cause triggering and duplicitous emotional responses, or worse yet, activation of internal mind control programming. That's when all hades breaks loose in the system and now the prayer session is in total chaos. The ministry that was taking place was now completely shut down and you're now focusing on shutting down the triggered programming.

When I work with survivors who are DID, I inform the family members to not allow any church members give the individual a prophetic word. The common response from the family member is, well, it's okay, because at our church we have a real prophet. Amazing how people who hear from God don't hear God tell them not to give false prophecy that hurts healing souls.

In the DID system, a lot of the identities are angry at God and want nothing to do with His presence. The parts haven't accepted their salvation, or they are even siding with demonic spirits. The parts are angry because they blame Jesus for not stopping the trauma and torture that happened to them. As you can see, a well-meaning prophetic word can cause utter chaos in a fractured soul. My ministry is a supernatural healing and inner healing ministry. I have prayed and have seen people healed from mental disorders and brain illnesses. DID is not a mental disorder, it is a fracturing of the soul. The soul is not flesh. It is non-corporeal. It is the human consciousness.

Healing comes when all the parts surrender to the love, grace, and mercy of Jesus Christ. In other words, each part must pick up its mat and walk. When this happens, Jesus brings the part back into the proper location of the soul for healing.

I have worked with some bipolar and DID individuals who obsessed over a false prophecy. Because the minister of the prophetic word was someone high in the Christian prophetic ministry circles, these afflicted souls just held onto the false prophecy. The DID soul will torment itself, for decades. when the prophetic word doesn't come to pass. There are a lot of dynamics going on here. In duplicitous programming, a part will constantly torment the Christian host that the prophetic word didn't transpire because Jesus doesn't love them. For the Christian host, this prophecy meant everything to him, but the word was from the minister's soul and not from God.

Remember the wise words of Saint Teresa of Avila? The problem with hearing from God is that man is fallible. It doesn't matter how respected the prophetic minister is in church circles, he is still a human being and imperfect. I rarely share any prophetic words in sessions. In deliverance and prayer ministry sessions, I only share the prophetic words the Holy Spirit instructs me to release. Many times the prophetic word I am instructed to give is to counter diseased attitudes. A good reason to share prophetic words, in this case, would be to break off self-condemnation. I would keep it very simple. And God the Father will keep it simple too. He wants to heal these broken souls and hearts.

Prophetic Words and Ritual Abuse Survivors

When you are working with ritual abuse survivors, the problem becomes tenfold because you are dealing with mind control programming. Even though the prayer recipient has a Christian host presenter, there are identities in the system programmed to counter the Christian host. This internal counter struggle is the duplicitous programming. This is one of the many reasons this ministry requires a lot of mentoring—you must be aware of the duplicitous parts operating in this form of severe bondage with double binds. The duplicitous part has the job of maintaining a state of hopelessness in the fractured soul system. As an example, I will use some prophetic ministry to work with a part that wants to meet and experience Jesus. Jesus will reveal some things unique to the part to enter into an encounter. A duplicitous part will be listening and start blasting the internal megaphone with blasphemous words about God and horrific, disgusting images depicting that part (note, don't confuse this with a blasphemous spirit which also shows up in normal deliverance ministry). The prophetic session gets shut down by the duplicitous part. This duplicitous interference happens frequently, but there are breakthroughs, and many times a duplicitous part is healed during Jesus encounters with other parts. Working with DID and trauma survivors takes a lot of time and patience. You can't have an agenda, and you must tread lightly and understand how and when to use prophetic ministry in sessions. For some people I work with, I won't use it at all because the duplicitous parts are hypervigilant. God still makes it to the parts. You just need to follow His lead and not get ahead of the healing.

A Case Example of Duplicitous Programming and Prophetic Ministry

A few years back, a friend and mentor of mine in street ministry, Pastor Bob, called me and asked me to speak to one of his interns, Tricia. Pastor Bob told me that the night before in a prophetic prayer session, Tricia had a powerful encounter with Jesus. The next day Tricia phoned Bob, and she was frantic on the phone call with him. She told Bob that dark principalities were going to kill her because of her experience with Jesus during the prayer session. Bob knows spiritual warfare, but when it's weird, he calls me. I knew Tricia because we had ministered before at outreaches, so Bob knew it would be okay for me to call her. I first sent a text message to Tricia asking her when would be a good time to call her. She replied back to my text message with the time I should call her. I then responded to Tricia's text message with, "Are you Tricia, or are you a part?" Tricia sent a text back to me with, "LOL – how did you know? Yes, I am a part."

How did I know I was communicating with an identity of Tricia? This odd situation required some prayer with Jesus. In my battles that involved angelic realms, not once was I in a confrontation with principalities simply because I had a powerful encounter with Jesus at a prayer meeting. The weight of the retaliation just didn't add up. The premise for retaliation against Tricia didn't make any sense. The high order satanic angels don't single out individual souls. They have low-order, low-pay-grade grunt demons to do that. I prayed to Jesus for revelation, and in a nutshell, He revealed to me that Tricia had a duplicitous part up that I needed to work with. Hence, the opening of the text message with, "Are you a part?" The duplicitous part came up and totally derailed Tricia's precious experience with Jesus. I was able to defuse the situation and let Tricia know that a duplicitous part made up the lie to wreck her powerful encounter with Jesus. With this revelation, I was able to minister to Tricia's duplicitous part and have it call off the lie of the principality's retaliation.

My Experience in Prophetic Ministry and with Duplicitous Parts

I would like to share with you one more story from the M16 Ministries X-files. This incident was a firsthand, gut-wrenching tribulation I experienced when giving a prophetic word to someone with a fractured soul. This event occurred earlier in my deliverance ministry walk. I didn't know what satanic ritual abuse was when this situation happened to me. Looking back, it demonstrates what can happen with a ritual abuse survivor in a friendly and safe spiritual prophetic setting. This account illustrates how something so good from God can go sideways so fast with a duplicitous part.

I was asked to give an equipping seminar on prophetic evangelism at a church in the San Francisco Bay area. It was a one-day training to launch ordinary people into prophetic street evangelism. It was a very successful event, and by the end of the day, some people in the class were testing out their skills in prophetic ministry. At the end of this seminar, I gave prophetic words to the attendees. One of the workshop participants was a woman named Danni. I gave Danni a prophetic word that a harsh season of life she was going through was now over. God said that she was about to enter into a new bountiful season of blessings. Simple prophetic word, the message being that bad things were now over, God's abundance and blessings were ahead. The prophetic word was very simple and straight-forward. Biblically it was sound, and it was an edifying word. The class was a success, and we all went home happy.

The very next morning, I got a call from the pastor of the church that held the seminar. The pastor told me that I needed to call Danni right away. The pastor said that he was furious at me for giving Danni a word that she was going to get cancer and die. I told the pastor that I had no clue of what Danni was talking about and that I didn't give her such a hor-rible word from God. He asked me to call her right away and straighten it out. I immediately called Danni, and she was crying on the phone. She told me she was so angry at me that I prophesied to her that she was going to get cancer and die. She was wailing over the phone and almost hung up on me. I told Danni that I was on my way to work and asked her if I could call her back that evening. I told her to throw away anything she thought she may have heard from me if it didn't align with the Holy Spirit. We teach our students that in giving and receiving prophetic words, they must line up with the Holy Spirit. If they don't, dispose of them. It's a simple way of testing the spirit.

Danni became furious at me and said how dare I tell her to throw away a word from God! I tried to explain to her that whatever was going on, if she knew the word she thought I'd given to her did not line up with the Holy Spirit, she should just discard it. Again, she came at me for being blasphemous and for asking her to disregard a prophetic word from God. There were signs of something not right, spiritually or mentally, with Danni. She would not reason with anything I had to say to her. I felt the evening would be a better time to work with her, and it would give me more time to understand what was going on. Better yet, she would have a full day to calm down.

As evening rolled around, and after I had dinner, my wife and I retired to our home office for phone calls and to wrap up some business for the day. I called Danni back, and she was even more fired up than previ-ously. She told me that she had a horrible day and was utterly miserable because I told her she was going to get cancer and die. I told Danni that was not the word I gave her, and I recited the word verbatim to her over the phone about entering into a new season of abundance and blessings. She screamed at me at the top over her lungs over the phone, "That is not what you said to me yesterday in the class, in front of all the people attending!"

I am going to throw in a spoiler here for your edification: can you see we're going in circles, and Danni won't budge from her state of mind? I didn't know what this was back then, but I do now. It is a duplicitous part that was interfering with Danni's spiritual development. I just wanted you to see how DID can go insanely in circles, but it isn't insanity! It's a part that is angry at Jesus and throws a temper tantrum. If you see this behavior in your deliverance or prophetic ministry, start shutting down whatever you are doing. As you can see, ministering to DID requires trained prayer ministers and counselors. This episode happened long before I had any experience with DID. Now back to retelling this account.

At this point, I switched the call over to speaker phone so my wife could hear the call. Danni was screaming into her cellphone. I asked Danni to calm down for a second so I could rewind this thing and bring it to a resolution. I told Danni that no matter what happened, I just wanted to take the time to own the whole situation and apologize and reboot. I proceeded to apologize to Danni when she interrupted and started screaming over my apology: "You listen to demons!" And she hung up the phone.

Lisa looked over at me after the call terminated. She didn't have to say a word; her expression said it all. Was the situation over? No! The very next day, Danni went into the senior pastor's office and continued to complain some more. Her duplicitous parts wanted retribution. The pastor should have handled the situation when the spirit of revenge reared its ugly little head. I received a call from the pastor, and he told me that I "threw a bad pitch" (i.e. bad prophetic word). I defended myself and told the pastor that I don't throw bad (prophetic) pitches. I had no intention of rebelling against his authority, but at the same time, I wasn't about to come into agreement with the lie of the enemy. The pastor became argumentative and embellished in pride over the phone. I was extremely disappointed with the pastor's discernment in this situation. We had a strong working relationship. He should have diffused the entire situation right there in his office. I was curious as to why the pastor and I were even having this conversation, since I had apologized to Danni the night before. I shared with the pastor that I had tried to make amends on the phone with Danni. The pastor refused to believe me and said that Danni had told him I didn't apologize, nor did I have any intention of apologizing to her. I had nothing further to add to the situation that was getting progressively worse. Are you beginning to see how the demonic can jump in and cause chaos with DID?

This confrontation with the pastor of this church was a very painful incident for me that left a gaping heart wound. Fascinating how demons infiltrate the church and initiate an offense that spreads quicker than a California wild grass fire. This incident demonstrates the dynamics of how a part angry at Jesus, in a Christian host, can partner with the demonic in seeking revenge. The enemy of my enemy is my friend holds true for angry duplicitous human parts. The enemy of the angry parts is Jesus. Classic DID dynamics are at play here. The part is seeking revenge for an incident it completely fabricated. A duplicitous part invented the lie, and another part is swallowed up in the deception.

Looking back, I know this happened for a reason. It showed me the respect and humility a minister must have for giving out prophetic words and also, the level of spiritual discernment a minister must operate at for prophetic and deliverance ministries. Both my wife and I could easily see through the demonic charade, but the pastor couldn't. Because it was demonic, I had to stand my ground, in humility, and let God vindicate me. Situations like this are why it is important to remain humble. This incident was one of my worst-case scenario learning experiences that I wish on no one. But it changed my way of thinking about how I deliver prophetic words. I experienced firsthand how fractured souls can twist a prophetic word and infiltrate demonic retribution inside the walls of the church. This incident occurred a month before I was supposed to lead a large prophetic evangelism team into a New Age expo outreach. I was the actual target of retribution of the enemy, and he started his bombing campaign against the outreach a month early. I was badly wounded going into the outreach from this incident. I had to fight off guilt, shame, and most of all, betrayal, as I prepared my soul to minister at this event. Never underestimate how much the enemy hates you in soul saving and deliverance ministry and how far he will go to stop you.

The experience at the New Age event lifted me up out of my spiritual dumps, and we had an amazing and successful time. The prophetic outreach team ministered to over two hundred people in one weekend, and there were no bizarre incidents of prophetic words going off track like they did with Danni. With hindsight being twenty-twenty, I now clearly understand that Danni was DID and most likely an SRA survivor. But I didn't understand what this was back then, nor did I have the ministry experience I have today that could have corrected the situation. Had this happened today, I would have brought Danni into counseling and gracefully triggered her parts to expose what she was trying to hide in her everyday life. These individuals already know they're DID, they just fear being mistaken for insane people or having their traumatized daily life exposed. I would have helped direct her to the long road of inner healing.

Lessons learned. God allows us to get sifted for a reason. I go through some strange seasons when God raises me in ministry. For me, there is a very thin line between a tribulation and a training season, so I don't recommend asking the Holy Spirit to receive training like I did. During this tribulation, I was allowed to minister to a fractured-demonized soul with prophetic ministry and experience firsthand the repercussions of the forces of darkness. The darkest trials will occur in the sanctity of the church and will leave you painfully isolated. It wouldn't be the last time I would work with demonized fractured souls.

Using Prophetic Ministry in DID Prayer Sessions

Do I use prophetic ministry with the people I pray with who are DID? Yes, because it is God that directs and brings their healing. I need to add here that my prophetic ministry operates under the utmost humility. I never say, "So sayeth the Lord," because I need to discern where the prophetic words are coming from: God, demons, or the soul. Use extreme caution and make sure you are in step with the Holy Spirit. Do I share with the people I am working with what God is saying? No, not all of the time. If the individual is hypervigilant, impatient, overly-religious, and trying to control his healing, I don't share prophetic information with him directly. I will filter it and release the prophetic word so it is subtle, and the person is unaware it is from God. Why do I do this? I am aware of duplicitous parts that will deliberately shut down the prayer session.

You must discern what God is showing you and what you should share. Some survivors obsess over everything shared with them, no matter how minor. There is no adjusting or correcting bad prophetic words given to them. Furthermore, I have found out that if I use prophetic ministry and give the prayer recipient a word from God, they will derail the prayer session and request more prophetic words. It's a way for duplicitous parts to interrupt the healing prayer session. Last of all, if you get a date and time someone will be healed from prophetic ministry, you are listening to your soul or a lying spirit. Only Jesus knows the timeline and He doesn't share it. It's His tactical information.

CHAPTER 11

Spiritual Afflictions

One of the biggest theological debates when it comes to demons is whether or not a Christian can have a demon. A false Christian doctrine in the Western world is that a Christian can't have a demon. The defining factor is that Christians have the Holy Spirit in them so they can't have a demon. This premise is valid to some extent. Remember, we are born into a fallen world. Our soul has a natural propensity to commit sin. I spoke earlier about sexual addiction. If a Christian man chooses to sin and sleep with a prostitute, he could likely expose himself in more ways than one to unclean spirits. He could sleep with a witch, knowingly or unknowingly. I have case histories for both and of people who got demonized by an incubus spirit. An incubus is a horrific raping spirit that manifests any time it wants and violates both the body and the soul. How did this man get demonized if he had the Holy Spirit in him? The Holy Spirit allows you to commit sin, no matter how stupid the action you desire to commit. The Holy Spirit didn't stop Adam and Eve in the garden of Eden. The Holy Spirit most likely convicted their hearts not to eat from the Tree of Knowledge of Good and Evil, but they did it regardless. The Holy Spirit grieves that you selected a stupid act of flesh over listening to Him. The Holy Spirit didn't force your soul to stop pursuing your sinful nature. Your soul committed sin of its own free will. Disregard to obedience to God always opens you up to very bad things.

You don't even have to go out of your way to have sex with a prostitute to get demonized. Ghost hunting, practicing yoga and Chi will also get you severely demonized. I have had long debates with Christians, and some with seminary PhDs, who don't understand how this demonization is possible. God allows the dog to return to its vomit.[1] Demonization happens most of the time through ignorant acts of the free will. Until you have worked a few cases involving these demonic oppressions, it won't make sense at all to you. Ignorance of God's laws, knowingly or unknowingly, will get you demonized. How is yoga a violation of God's laws? Jesus told us that the most important commandment is to love your God with all your heart and all your mind and all your strength. Yoga is a practice of the Hindu religion, the worship of false gods that are demons. Wait a minute? Isn't Yoga a multi-billion-dollar health industry here in America? Yes, it is. But again, yoga is Hinduism and every posture in yoga is in adoration to a Hindu demon. Don't fall into the deceptive ideology trap that yoga can undergo a Christian makeover. Demons can't be redeemed, nor can anything that comes from their labor. Yoga can't be redeemed and with it comes curses. I don't usually speak strongly against things like this unless I have worked with the demonic activity firsthand.

Too many Christians are academic spiritual warfare experts. This is as useful as sending soldiers to war who read about shooting a gun but never actually fired one. They head to the battlefield considering themselves to be experts. This scenario is the state of spiritual warfare in the Western church today.

Christians are not immune to demonic oppression or possession. There is a difference between the two. Christians tend to see demonic oppression and possession as the same thing. One root cause of this misconception may be from the King James Version of the Holy Bible. The King James translation has its strengths and weaknesses when it comes to spiritual warfare. Where the translation is weak is in its definition of possession. Nearly all the demonic accounts in the King James Version of the Bible call demonic oppression *possession*. This translation is highly

---

1 Proverbs 26:11

inaccurate because possession means the spirits are in complete control of the soul and the body. Let's look at a verse describing Jesus healing an afflicted soul from two different translations of the Bible. The first verse is from the King James Version of the Bible: "As they went out, behold, they brought to him a dumb man possessed with a devil" (Matthew 9:32 KJV), in comparison to the Aramaic English New Testament (AENT) translation of the same verse: "And when Y'shua went out, they brought a mute to him that had a demon in him" (Matthew 9:32 AENT).

Other translations use the word *demoniac* which is slightly better. At least the word demoniac suggests there are different levels of demonic oppression. There is a difference between an oppressed demoniac and a possessed demoniac in the Bible. The Gospels give us understanding on the levels of oppression, from lesser demonic affliction making a man mute to the most severe case of the possession of a man in the story of the Gerasene demoniac. The King James Version translation leads the reader to believe that all demoniacs are under possession by evil spirits.

Possessed or oppressed: A demonic oppression is when the demon isn't always present and most of the time can afflict the soul from a distance (think inter-dimensional) or in the body. Christian souls can be severely afflicted and oppressed by a demon—the spirit attacks with physical illness, locutions, manifestations, and uses of their bodies. Some oppressions can be so severe that they appear to be possession. Spiritual oppression is the most common suffering of demoniacs in the Bible. The individual can pray, petition Jesus for help, and fight back yet be severely oppressed by the demon. In contrast, the possessed individual has no control over his thoughts or actions. The most severe state for a demoniac is possession. There are different levels of demonic torment and how the soul is afflicted.

A Case of Christian Possession

A few years back I was attending a church on a Sunday morning. The senior pastor had just invited the Holy Spirit to manifest his presence in the sanctuary. When the Holy Spirit moved into the house of worship, a demoniac in the congregation started screaming out. The spectacle was a young woman in her thirties named Stacey. She was shaking violently and screaming out in agony when the Holy Spirit manifested his presence. The chaos was disrupting the church service.

People kept looking over at me to do something, but I was not on staff at this church, so I sat there waiting to be released into ministry. Finally a friend of mine, Pastor Jimi, asked me to come over and assist with the demonic manifestation. Jimi and I have done numerous deliverances together. After being released into ministry by Pastor Jimi, I walked over and put my hand over Stacey's forehead, and I prayed to bind her occult third eye to close. Why did I do this? Because as I sat waiting to be released, or not be released, into ministry, the Holy Spirit shared with me that this was a spirit of the occult. Once the third eye closed, I prayed to bind the demon to silence. After this Stacey immediately stopped shaking and screaming. Jimi and I then led the woman out to a prayer room where we interviewed her as to what was going on.

Stacey was still trembling, confused, and highly embarrassed from her public spectacle in the church service. Jimi's wife, Holly, joined us for the interview session. Stacey's heart rate slowly returned to a normal state and she began to reveal to us what was going on. She explained that a few years previously, she was very sick and almost died. Stacey was a survivor of a life-threatening cancerous disease that tried to ravage her muscle tissue and her bones. A leading Northern California university hospital in the San Francisco Bay area recommended that Stacey look into practicing yoga. Stacey was introduced to yoga very innocently as a healthy lifestyle change. Beware of the occult, the wolf in sheep's clothing. The occult has infiltrated our healthcare system and our healthy living.

Stacey was willing to do whatever it took to fight for her life and followed the new medical advice and took up yoga. She fully embraced it and wanted to learn everything she could about yoga, so much so that she even went to India to study under a yogi for several weeks. She studied the ancient Sanskrit, and in her grand moment of practicing yoga, Stacey achieved the spiritual activation of her Kundalini. For Stacey, she described it as a very violent experience. She said she shook, then her legs threw themselves apart in a forceful manner, and she urinated on herself.

Stacey said that her body trembled there for a while. The experience happened to her several times during her yoga spiritual road trip in India.

What Stacey didn't bargain for was that the experience followed her home. Every time she tried to pray to God or study her Bible, she would feel her legs wanting to throw themselves apart, and she knew she would be urinating on herself almost immediately. She found herself bolting to the bathroom to finish her prayer time. The Kundalini rooted itself as a lying spirit, making Stacey believe it was the Holy Spirit powerfully manifesting inside of her. Every time Stacey wanted to have deep prayer, she had to do so in the bathroom to prepare for the inevitable.

When I worked with Stacey on the fact that the Kundalini was acting like a lying spirit, she refused to listen to the truth. In fact, the lying spirit had already got to work on deceiving her about her spiritual beliefs. After our interview with Stacey concluded, I felt an exorcism was in order. We were dealing with a Christian that was demonically possessed and she had invited in her unwanted captors. I required another meeting with Stacey.

During this second meeting session, I planned to do an exorcism with Stacey. Things didn't go that way, though. The lying spirit had a plan of its own. I asked Pastor Jimi's wife, Holly, to join me in this session. In our meeting, Stacey showed me the information she had gathered from Sanskrit (liturgical prayers of Hinduism) experts at the University of California, Berkeley, saying that Sanskrit was older than Jesus. The lying spirit denied Jesus being the creator of the universe, the one who was God incarnate, and the savior.

The lying religious spirit manifested during the session and spouted off about how Jesus was only a person who lived two thousand years ago. Remember, Stacey was a practicing Catholic and was raised in the church. She knew the way, the truth, and the light. As a possessed demoniac, she was saying whatever the religious spirit wanted her to say. The lying spirit continued to tell us that the Sanskrit was true and Jesus was a myth. Despite Stacey's catechism teachings, the demon's lies were weaving their thick web of deceit. I reminded Stacey of the truth from the Gospel of John that in the beginning was the Word, and the Word is Jesus

Christ. She continued to argue that counterpoint of the Sanskrit. Stacey's spiritual weakness would be troubling for the exorcism. I was counting on her faith in Jesus Christ, but her spiritual authority had now submitted itself to the deception of her demons. My next plan of attack was to pray and see if the spirit would manifest in the counseling office with Holly and me. I prayed and asked for the presence of the Holy Spirit to manifest. Holly and I laid hands on Stacey and waited for the Holy Spirit to manifest. Stacey started getting this dramatic, joyous look on her face, and she said that she could feel the Holy Spirit's presence. At the same moment, I could discern through my smelling senses the scent of burning sulfur. My spiritual discernment revealed it wasn't the Holy Spirit at all. The lying spirit was deceiving Stacey to stop her from being freed in the prayer session. To make matters even more problematic, Stacey didn't want to be set free from the spirit of Kundalini and the other spirits possessing her. She had sought out and given the spirit of Kundalini permission, called *subjugation*, to enter her. Stacey is a case example of Christian demonic possession.

I told Stacey she needed to abandon her yoga interests. She didn't want to listen. I told her I could forward her case to a local Roman Catholic diocese exorcist, since she was Roman Catholic. Stacey didn't want to listen to anything I had to say, and for a week or so afterward, Stacey e-mailed me deceptive articles on Christian yoga she'd found on the Internet about how safe it was.

Stacey wasn't the only case I have seen with the demonic spirit of Kundalini. I have seen more disturbing possessions that cause the eyes to roll in the back of the head and make people levitate. The Kundalini spirit is a demon. Demons are unredeemable and so is everything associated with them. Any church that has yoga in it needs to follow the greatest commandment and get rid of it! Yoga is present in church sanctuaries because of the participators' ignorance to the law of God and severe lack of spiritual discernment. The Hindu demons defile God's sanctuary. Yoga is no more welcome in God's church than an Asherah pole. With defilement comes judgment and curses! Can a Christian be possessed? Absolutely! God will let us do anything we want in our fallen nature, but not without consequences for our behavior. He will let us roam into darkness and get demonized, but if we repent from this sin, He will also take us back.

Oppression

The most common form of affliction on the soul is demonic oppression. A demonic oppression is the sign of a definitive attack on the soul. Oppression can vary greatly, from a person feeling like he's having a highly unusual bad day to the worst case which is a spirit manifesting in a person. Through oppression, spirits can speak to us through internal voices called *locutions* and interject evil thoughts to us. Demons can influence our soul through the intellect, will, imagination, and memories. With a bad day, demons can compound things with negative thoughts, false offenses, or even paranoia. Nobody on this earth is safe from spiritual oppression. These attacks are called *demonic torment*. With severe cases of demonic oppression, a soul can be physically attacked by unseen forces.

With demonic oppression, the demon may or may not be in the oppressed soul's body. However, the spirit will be able to draw up memories of condemnation, build a stronghold (which is a definitive sign of demonic oppression), and may even be able to take over parts of the body and mind. Through demonic oppression, the individual doesn't necessarily have to have a doorway open that is allowing the demons access. A generational curse can give a demon what it feels is legal access to even the most devout Christian. The late Padre Pio, a Christian mystic in the Catholic Church, went on to his glory in the 1960s. He was a devout Catholic priest who underwent excruciating diabolic oppression and torment. As far as I know, Padre Pio didn't have any doors open to the demonic. What if you were going about your own business in elementary school and the school bullies decided to pounce you? And then this went on every day for a week until you stood up to them and it stopped. Some demonic oppressions are like this.

I have a friend named Craig. He and his wife are incredible deliverance ministers. Craig undergoes horrific succubus attacks and torment. Keep in mind that God is a mystery. We don't know why these attacks happen with Craig. Other ministers, Roman Catholic exorcists, and I have broken every curse fathomable. I am apprehensive about mentioning Craig's case. He is one of a few people who actually has something really weird going on. Why I am apprehensive about sharing this is because I will get a lot of e-mails from people stating they are in Craig's situation but they are not. They're listening to lying spirits and being deceived into avoiding taking responsibility for their lives. I mention Craig here because it shows what sort of open mind we must have when we work with people. In Craig's case, it could very well be some Job-like tribulation.

The primary method a demon uses to oppress a Christian is through the building of strongholds in the soul. A common tactic of the enemy is to create offense with another human being. Have you ever noticed when you are deep in spiritual warfare, the enemy uses family, friends, and church members to create offense with you? The enemy knows how to use an offense as a nuclear weapon in his retaliation against your spiritual warfare.

The second most common method a spirit oppresses through is a generational curse or inherited sin. The curse is an iniquity which could have been in the family bloodline for several generations. During deliverance sessions, these spirits can surface inside a body and speak. Keep in mind these are common demonic oppressions that afflict the believer's soul. Nowhere in the Bible does it say that a Christian can't have a demon.

Another common way we can become oppressed is through our poor judgment. We have free will and God allows us to do some dumb things. We curse ourselves with our personal sin. Examples of things Christians commonly do that offend God and open demonic doors are: being involved in New Age meditation, Chi, yoga, divination, and ghost hunting. I've had to clean up severe demonic oppression off every Christian ghost hunter I ever knew. They picked up hitchhiking ghosts, called *spiritual attachments*. Ghost hunting, let's call it by its real name: Spiritism; and recording disembodied voices (necromancy) are abominations to God.

> *When you enter the land which the Lord your God gives you, you shall not learn to imitate the detestable things of those nations. There shall not be found among you anyone who makes*

his son or his daughter pass through the fire, one who uses divination, one who practices witchcraft, or one who interprets omens, or a sorcerer, or one who casts a spell, or a medium, or a spiritist, or one who calls up the dead. For whoever does these things is detestable to the Lord; and because of these detestable things the Lord your God will drive them out before you.

—Deuteronomy 18:9-12

Intercessors and prayer warriors can experience attacks of oppression while praying for others. Some intercessors falsely believe they have an anointing to battle in heavenly realms. The heavens belong to the Lord, and any intercessor that battles in the heavenly places is operating dangerously with no covering. Even though the enemy is unseen, it does fight back. I carefully select my intercessors and train them to be aware of the danger of engaging in warfare in the heavens. When battling the occult, the oppression can get pretty severe. Only have people on your intercessory team you can trust and who don't create unnecessary battles for you.

Spiritual Attachment

Somewhere between demonic oppression and demonic possession is spiritual attachment. Christians can pick up spiritual attachments by living in homes with demonic activity. Playing with Ouija boards commonly creates spiritual attachments. Spirits want to inhabit people and animals. In homes with activity, the spirits will want to interact with the people living in or visiting these spaces. Nothing good comes from spiritual attachment. It is a spiritual oppression that can lead to severe demonic oppressions, like a demonic obsession. In more extreme cases it can lead from obsession to possession.

I was brought in on one case by my friend Sonia. She was working with a Christian teen girl who was battling spiritual attachment. Sonia invited me out to walk the girl's house with her to get a feel of the activity in this environment. During my initial walk through the house I sensed an infuriated spirit at the foot of the stairway on the second-floor of the house. The Holy Spirit revealed to me a picture of a spirit of addiction.

I told Sonia about the revelation I got of some old drug-addicted guy who would march back and forth at the top of the stairs enraged. Sonia mentioned she had picked up the same thing on her initial walk through of this house. When I interviewed the young girl, who lived upstairs, she told me about a dark mass that would manifest at night above her bed. The young Christian woman was experiencing spiritual attachment. Sonja and I taught her basic spiritual warfare, and the young teen girl reclaimed her room. In this case, the unclean spirit was trying to attach itself to the young woman spiritually. She resisted and fought back. Victory only comes by standing in your spiritual authority!

I worked with a young Christian woman a year ago who volunteered to go out with a paranormal team to bless a house. Perfectly innocent intentions, but she participated more out of curiosity than in acting as a prayer minister. She got caught up in the thrill of the hunt and ended up bringing home a hitchhiking spirit. She came to me for deliverance prayer, and she was pretty much excited with her real experience in deliverance and prophetic ministry. More so, she didn't need to return to ghost hunting. She discovered her new passion in Jesus and his ministry. You can experience God without going to hauntings and listening to EVPs (electric voice phenomena). Ghost hunting experiences have nothing to do with God or give proof of his existence. And foremost, those things are detestable to God!

During house blessings, a spiritual attachment can occur. The spirit gets evicted but may follow you home. I have experienced this once on a missionary trip, and over the period of a week, I saw a shadow figure I expelled from a house. The spirit followed me to places where I was staying. The spirit was finally completely removed and expelled by the end of the week. Why had it followed me around? I don't know. The only thing I can figure was that it needed more prayers to be completely banished, so it somehow got spiritually handcuffed to me. Never put God in a box; we never know how he is going to resolve a situation.

The dangers of spiritual attachment are that they can easily become a demonic obsession or even possession if not dealt with immediately. Severe spiritual attachment is what ghost hunters call *partial possession*.

That is, the attached spirit can manifest in the person and overwhelm the emotions. The attack on the emotions is an attack on his human spirit. Many television ghost hunters suffer from severe spiritual attachment, and the spirits appear to them nightly. The Ghost Adventures television crew are very outspoken about the attacks on them. The spirits even went after their wives, family members, and children. Makes you wonder why they do what they do. I would guess that they are so obsessed with this activity that they can't stop themselves. During demonic obsession, the will becomes compromised. By the way, if you are a ghost hunter, oppression is inevitable. Through oppression the spirits are given legal rights to oppress your blood lines for generations.

Obsession

With obsession, the demonic attacks keep the person obsessively focused on the torment. The soul is distracted away from being Christ-centric and focused on the demonic activity around him. In this way, he is distracted from his prayer life and relationship with Jesus Christ. The person isn't standing in his spiritual authority in Jesus Christ. Usually by the time the oppression turns to obsession, the person isn't responding to any spiritual advice at all. In cases of obsession, the demons increase their attacks of paranoia, hallucinations, and hearing voices to drive the person to the point of wanting to commit suicide.

Obsession can occur from living in a defiled house (either haunted or just a spiritually oppressed atmosphere from the previous tenants) where a tragic event such as molestation; addiction; suicide; emotional, physical, sexual, or ritual abuse occurred. The sad thing about obsession is that people caught up in it eventually find themselves strapped to a hospital gurney at the county hospital mental ward—if they don't seek the proper help. For some strange reason, one of the end goals of obsession is to make the individual look insane. The demons will torment the individual when he is alone and isolated, so activity is rarely ever witnessed by others. A soul trapped in the obsession will have strange behaviors like pointing out demons no one else can see. I had cases where people were obsessed with taking pictures and recordings of spirits speaking with their phones. This behavior was a nonstop obsession: all they could do all day was to seek proof of what was happening to them. The soul is focused only on the demonic activity around him. Their spiritual alignment is completely inverted away from Christ. Obsession is a step closer to demonic possession. I think this is the reason the spirits try to push the soul's intellect to the point of appearing or becoming insane. Ever wonder what happens when those prayers to see angels get answered? This is a crucial reason why one shouldn't pray to see angels or demons. God won't answer that prayer, but something else will. And once you give the spirits legal rights to torment you with obsession, it is difficult to shut down. One minute you want to see spirits, which you think is the answer to your prayer, and the next minute you can't stop seeing spirits everywhere. The will of the soul is compromised and can't do anything but focus on the supernatural events around it. Shutting down obsession is a long road of steering the soul back to focus on Jesus. Many times this seems impossible, and you have to wait for the soul to wake up from its torment. A lot of intercession is required to wake these individuals up. Many people stuck in obsession think a deliverance session will undo everything. Not so! Jesus must walk the soul out of demonic obsession. It takes as long as it takes. The obsessed souls usually get fed up with the long healing process and think they need to find another deliverance minister. Beware of the people who come to you with an extensive list of other deliverance ministers they have already seen. If they are obsessed, your ministry is yet another road stop to another deliverance ministry. An obsessed soul needs to wake up from his obsession.

Working with individuals who are demonically obsessed requires that you set boundaries with them right away. These are the types of cases where the people will call you every hour on the hour to report in on what is going on with them. When it gets to this point, I let the Holy Spirit tell me when it is time to answer the phone or text back. Obsessive behavior is an effective tactic the enemy uses to wear down the prayer ministry team. I don't give out the number of my intercessors to anyone. I am the point of contact. One obsessed soul can wear down and obliterate an entire intercessory team with his behavior. I also don't allow the obsessive cases to make requests for prayer. The obsessed individual does it your way or they can hit the highway. And that's no empty threat.

Possession

Christians tend to throw around the phrase "demon possessed" without clearly understanding the meaning. I will get phone calls from concerned Christians stating that a person they know at church is demon possessed. This will sound odd to me, because a person that is demon possessed will not attend church! In my case history, maybe once every so often do I get an actual demonic possession case. I get a lot of severe demonic oppression cases that resemble possession to the unequipped, average churchgoer. The apostle Mark accurately depicted a demonic possession with his account of the Gerasene demoniac.

> When he got out of the boat, immediately a man from the tombs with an unclean spirit met him, and he had his dwelling among the tombs. And no one was able to bind him anymore, even with a chain; because he had often been bound with shackles and chains, and the chains had been torn apart by him and the shackles broken in pieces, and no one was strong enough to subdue him. Constantly, night and day, he was screaming among the tombs and in the mountains, and gashing himself with stones.

—Mark 5:2-5

In my experiences with the possessed demoniacs, it pretty much matches up with what the Bible describes. The possessed have no free will whatsoever in their soul. A possessed soul is a completely compromised will, intellect, and imagination of the mind. The individual behaves like a lunatic and has an aversion to Christian objects, Bibles, and sacraments. A possessed soul would not enter a church under its own free will. Many times, the possessed person will demonstrate supernatural behaviors, such as knowledge about you that is impossible to know. The person may suddenly speak different languages he doesn't know. A possessed person can exhibit supernatural activity (things out of the norm, lights flickering when they enter a room, levitation, teleportation) and have many spirits talking out of them. I have witnessed levitation, and one time I witnessed teleportation.

When I witnessed levitation, it was done by a yoga instructor at Burning Man. Our ministry team had a tent people could enter to hear a word from their creator. Two yogis came and sat down on the carpet at my feet. My team members with me called on the Spirit of Truth, the Holy Spirit, and these guys went into a trance, their eyeballs rolled back, and they went flat on their backs. One of the yogis looked up at me and let out a scream. His upper body started levitating off the ground. I bound the spirit and he fell flat back on the ground. We just prayed over the yogis until their manifestations stopped. They got up and walked away. Before they did, they asked us what power we were tapping into because they could feel that the power inside them was afraid of it. Welcome, to the crazy Burning Man encounters we have. It's a pagan festival, so we're going to run into quite a few demons. The two yogis were under full possession by spirits of Kundalini. And those spirits in the yogis didn't want to be in a tent full of "Book of Acts" walking Christians and an exorcist.

When you encounter demonic possession, the person's free will is completely compromised and the spirits are in control. It is possession of the will and body (not the spirit). God created us in his likeness with a body, a mind, and a spirit. The Holy Spirit inhabits our human spirit while the demons try to invade the soul and body. Dealing with demonic possession is beyond the ministry of deliverance. It requires real exorcism warriors set apart by God. These battles are long term and can be violent. If you don't understand battles with the occult and in the heavenly realms, do not take on these cases. Seek a ministry that does and connect with them for assistance. Dealing with demonic possession can wipe out a ministry and a church. Sadly, a lot of inexperienced deliverance ministries pass themselves off as being experienced and experts in this subject matter and they are not. Use your discernment and test the spirit on these teams. Even when you find the right ministry, the minister must consult the heavenly Father for permission to engage the enemy.

Subjugation is a form of demonic possession I commonly encounter with former occult members. In this form of possession, the soul freely gave itself over to Satan in rituals. Setting a soul free from subjugation is intense and at times violent. Any and all forms of possession require an exorcist for ministry.

Pray to Be Released into Dark Battles

If someone comes to you with a demonic possession case, make sure you have the right team to handle it. When I do a consultation in occult cases, I tell people I will give them my answer in a week. The possession has been going on for a while, so a week will be nothing. I need the solitude to consult with my heavenly Father. If I get the go ahead, I have all the resources in heaven backing me up. Remember, operate in humility first and wait for God to speak to you. He may tell you not to take the case. Do what God the Father says.

When I worked my very first SRA case, two days afterward I was contacted by a possessed man in my area to help him. I told the man I would pray about it. He got upset with me. But too bad, that's how I operate in ministry. I contacted my close friend Pastor Jimi to pray with me for checks and balances on what I was hearing from God. I heard in my spirit, over the course of the next two days, that I was not to contact this man any further and to drop the case. I checked in with Pastor Jimi, and he said he felt, in the spirit, it was a trap. The man wanted to get me out to his house and let his demons beat me up. I wasn't afraid at all. We both heard from God not to take the case. We used God's covering, and we only go where God sends us. When the Father tells me no, I obey!

When you take on a case of demonic possession, as I have demonstrated, you and your prayer team must be able to hear from God. You must have an intercessory team that understands not to war in the heavens and why we don't bind Satan. Your prayer team members must have an understanding of the occult and the supernatural. The prayer team must not be in any stage of addictive sin or behavioral sin. I am not saying that they don't sin, I am outlining the character of the prayer warrior. Are they walking with God to be righteous? The most horrific attacks come with dealing with the occult and possession. By horrific, I don't mean manifestations at their homes, which can happen. I am talking about the destruction of families and marriages. How solid are the marriages of your team members? How covered in prayer are the family members, pets, properties, and households? Intercessory prayer warriors are not your average church intercessory team members, and not everyone is cut out for this prayer team because of the way the occult battles against them. How do you build these teams? You build the team over time and pick up other gunfighters along the way.

For my first demonic possession case, I prayed for at least three months. That's how long it took before the heavenly Father gave me the okay to engage the enemy. When I first met this young man, Trevor, we couldn't get him into the church for the exorcism. His mom would bring him and Trevor would bolt out of the church during the prayers of liberation. I didn't want to restrain this person at all. The only thing we could do was pray and intercede. Demonic possession is really strange. Trevor kept switching spirits as we tried to minister to him. Some spirits came up and told us they were the ones the Mayans sacrificed their babies to. Then the next second spirits came up and said they were the ones who fly through the rings of Saturn. It was clearly a demonic possession. The trapped soul had no will to speak for itself whatsoever. Trevor was a Christian who had become angry at God for the untimely deaths of his father and older brother. As an act of revenge, Trevor sold his soul to Satan. This young man was a Christian until his life was devastated by the deaths in his family. He blamed God.

For over a month or longer, we prayed for liberation through an intercessory team. Then one day, the Father released us into battle. When the day came, the young man walked into the church under his free will, received the liberation prayers, and was set free. The timeline was close to three months from when we met the demoniac to when he was finally prayed for and set free. The Holy Spirit did all the work and we stayed in intercession waiting to hear from the Father. Trevor was a case of subjugation. He freely gave his soul over to Satan.

Praying to be released into battle is imperative. You must bridle your pride and let the Holy Spirit do all the work in these dark battles. I am always amazed at what God shows me through these experiences. Always listen to what God is telling you. Never step out from underneath his covering!

Discerning the Type of Affliction

The Holy Spirit will train you over time and put you through seasons of types of warfare. I remember when the Holy Spirit trained me for demonic obsession warfare, I was bewildered by the strangeness of this soul affliction. I couldn't understand how it was that a soul got to this point. But that wasn't what I was brought in to pontificate. God wanted to show me how to work with the demonically obsessed. I had a season of nothing but demonically obsessed cases coming to me. That's how the Holy Spirit trained me. You let God show you what is going on in front of you and how you should work with Him. God will bring in confusion to train you. It is His way of showing you that He brings healing and not you. But after you go through seasons of things like this, you are better able to identify what the affliction is. You will get things wrong too. We're not perfect. But the Holy Spirit is training you. I went through a similar season with the SRA cases, only this season wasn't months, it was years. How long does it take for the Holy Spirit to train you? However long it takes!

Keep in mind that discernment comes through just being a seasoned warrior. Demonic obsession and dissociative identity disorder can look very similar. But once you've been through those training seasons with the Holy Spirit, you can start spotting various afflictions a mile away!

CHAPTER 12

Spiritual Manifestations

I n this section, we're going to discuss some spiritual behaviors you
will undoubtedly encounter in your warfare ministry sessions. The
following information comes firsthand from my knowledge base
in operating in this ministry for the past ten years. When I presented
this information in the original Front Lines of Spiritual Warfare course,
this was the favorite section for pastoral staff. The information and
testimonies come from my encounters in ministry with the real unseen
dimension of God's spiritual realm.

Much of what I present is my interpretation of what I perceived to
have occurred through various ministry sessions over the years. Because
it comes from man, me, this information is fallible. I want to say that up
front. As a word of advice, turn and run away from anyone who claims to
be an expert in this field. Spiritual manifestations take us into the study
of mystical theology. God is a mystery. He brings the final revelation on
the content I present below through His Holy Spirit.

Discernment of Spirits

Before I address the various topics in manifestations, I would like to give
a quick overview of spiritual discernment. A seasoned deliverance minister is pretty open to mystical experiences and supernatural discernment
responses in his body. By this I mean the body is an excellent radar for
discerning the presence of spirits. Since we are spiritual beings embodied

in flesh, the unseen reality of the spirit realm can be picked up by our spirit and the information can be transmitted to our body's physical sensory receptors of touch, feeling, sight, hearing, and smell.

Before a demon manifests, your body can detect the presence of the unclean spirit. When I work with people in deliverance, I always pause and ask the people on my team what they are feeling at the moment I sense a manifestation. Many times, I will first feel a sensation of pressure on my chest. The slight chest pressure is the armor of God alerting me to a manifestation. When I have my seasoned crew working with me, I will lightly tap my chest when I have their attention. I will get an affirmative nod back that they are feeling it too. When I experience the start of a manifestation, I don't want the prayer recipient to know what I am detecting. These are kind of like quick baseball hand signals to my team. At this point the deliverance team knows a spirit is present. It may not have manifested yet, but something came to the party. Discerning spirits is crucial in deliverance ministry.

How can you learn about your discernment? You can do simple exercises to develop your spiritual discernment. One thing my wife and I like to do is go to open homes for sale in and around our neighborhood to get upgrade ideas for our home. It's common for me, when I enter homes, to feel the oppression. It's tangible. The oppression may come as a feeling that there is something not right with the house. I will then walk the house and let my body be a compass to show me where the fingerprint of oppression is in the home. It's like using your body to play the kids' game "hot or cold." As your body dials in on the oppression, you call out, "Getting warmer." If you walk in one direction and the oppression weakens, you would call out, "Getting colder." I don't call out "hotter" or "colder." I just use this game to illustrate how to use your body's spiritual discernment in an oppressed house. The technique is similar when I walk through a home with demonic activity.

During one particular open home walkthrough, Lisa and I were in a beautiful hundred-year-old cottage in our neighborhood. We walked the house to tour it and see the graceful century-old architecture. When we made our way upstairs, my Spidey sense, aka my discernment, went off.

I let my body guide me to the room with spiritual activity. I called out to my wife, "Hey Lisa, come here and check this out!" Lisa walked in from the other room, then her Spidey sense triggered. She said, "Oh wow! I can feel that!"

The real estate agent listing the home was hot on the heels of Lisa when I called out to her. She thought she had a buyer. The woman walked in and heard Lisa's comment and said, "Feel what?" I moved in with damage control and commented on the paint scheme, which was nothing spectacular. The realtor just gave us a puzzled look and departed.

Other warning triggers of manifestations include uneasiness in the stomach, and sometimes a quickly oncoming, nasty migraine headache. Since I am not prone to having migraines, I can pick up on this one right away. Many times, the source of a migraine is from spirits calling on the power of witchcraft to engage you in battle, but not always. Bind witchcraft immediately when you feel it. You'll notice your headache begin to diminish immediately in the prayer session.

> *In the authority of Jesus Christ, I bind the witchcraft, and I*
> *bind the spirits from calling out to higher powers.*

When I was in Cambodia in 2015, I was visiting an orphanage with a team of missionaries who had just completed training at a well-known school of supernatural ministry. I entered the orphanage and instantly felt sick to my stomach, like I wasn't going to make it to the bathroom. Then I could feel something demonic. I stepped back off the threshold of the orphanage's front door to get some sort of spiritual baseline measurement for myself. Outside the doorway threshold, I was perfectly fine. I stepped over the threshold, I felt sick. I dismissed myself from the nickel tour the orphanage was giving and asked for permission to walk the house. I went upstairs and could feel the areas of oppression in the headmistress's bedroom quarters. The orphanage had a balcony, and I stepped out on it, where I heard an internal spiritual locution telling me to jump off. I knew then I had an unclean spirit in the house. I walked the rest of the upstairs and I could feel the areas where the spirit was tormenting some children at night.

Later that evening, the ministers asked me how come they couldn't feel the presence in the same way I could. I believe that since part of my ministry involves battling the occult on nearly a daily basis, feeling manifestations is almost like a trained muscle reflex.

When I interviewed the headmistress of the orphanage, she told me an incredible story of how a headless shadow would come through the wall and go over to the kids' sleeping quarters and shake their bunkbeds violently. The headmistress explained to me how the bed shaking had stopped—she was taking authority over the demon to expel it. One of the helpers to the headmistress was a former Buddhist. She witnessed the spiritual authority of the Christian headmistress and decided firsthand that this Christianity thing was real! There was some warfare still going on when I arrived on the scene. I was amazed at how these Christian women were dealing with it. They were pushing back on the enemy hard, and the demonic was losing ground. Over a timeframe of a week, I worked in prayer and Holy Spirit meditation to exorcise the spirit from the orphanage.

What about seeing demonic spirits? On occasion, God will allow you to see in the spirit through His grace. It is not something we ask Him to reveal to us. On occasion, I will see spirits, but not often. I am highly skeptical of the number of deliverance ministers who claim to see spirits all the time. There are a few souls I know who can, but the others I believe are soulishly promoting this deception to advance their ministries. You can't operate a deliverance ministry on deceit and pride or you will be called out by the demons. Many times the people I have worked with who claimed to see spirits frequently in deliverance sessions were either lying or were being spiritually oppressed and attacked. Never fake discernment. This ministry is full of mystical testimonies and healings. There is no need to falsify evidence or discernment. The ministry is not for the fake-it-until-you-make-its. People coming to you for ministry are already hurting. Unfortunately, I must undo a lot of bad deliverance ministry in counseling sessions with survivors of severe trauma.

Discernment is given through God's grace. He will allow us to experience mystical experiences and discernment as He sees fit. He is God the Father, and He knows what's best for us.

Manifestations and Outsourcing Their Sanctification

All manifestations are mystical experiences that occur under the grace and mercy of God. They can happen in a prayer ministry time, but that's not what happens all the time. People may contact you and out of desperation wanting to convince you that they need to meet and have demonic influences driven from them. Always be the skeptic and make them prove to you that they are dealing with something demonic.

Not everyone that comes to you will be demonically afflicted. Many will be self-afflicted souls suffering from the sin of their ungodly lifestyles. They need to be told to take responsibility for their behaviors. Always bring the compassion of Jesus Christ into the situation. If a demon manifests during the interview, then there's your proof. The number one rule about demons is that they want to remain hidden. A demon may not manifest during your meeting. Developing your spiritual discernment is critical. Let the Holy Spirit reveal the presence of a demon. Rely on your discernment and not the person requesting prayer. I quietly ask my prayer team what they are discerning. Ministry takes time, so have no agenda on these matters.

If a manifestation does occur, this is not a sign of demonic possession. Demons can manifest in Christians who have a demonic oppression. A generational curse can manifest if it is present in the family line. A Christian living in a spiritually tainted home can have a spiritual attachment speak through him. However, this isn't always the case.

What I have found is that many Christians are just giving the devil too much credit. Sometimes we just want to believe a situation is demonic so we can simply have a deliverance minister make it go away. The fact of the matter is, deliverance ministers don't bring any healing, only Jesus does. But on a subconscious level, we fear the truth. The Holy Spirit is in charge of the deliverance ministry session. Whatever "lie" the prayer recipient is harboring or suppressing will reveal itself.

About a year ago I was contacted by a gentleman named Tim who lived relatively near me, but he found me through a deliverance minister out of state. Tim was frantic when he contacted me. He was partially blind, and he believed the house he lived in had demonic activity. He said the demon would follow him everywhere he moved. He said the demon cursed him with poor health. Tim's body was ill, and he felt his case had met all the criteria for a deliverance ministry session.

I decided to set up a deliverance session in a church near his house. I had a good friend and mentor, Pastor Earl, who graciously, allowed me to use his church. The bonus to this session was that Pastor Earl was going to minister with me. I always love to work with seasoned pastors who are great and compassionate ministers like Pastor Earl. You get to learn a thing or two as well when you work with men like this.

With all the things Tim told us were going on with him, our ministry team thought for sure there would be a manifestation during the session. There was no manifestation during the entire session. Earl and I prayed for some time simply for the presence of the Holy Spirit to increase in the room and for His revelation to come. Nothing happened at all, other than the room became very peaceful with the presence of God. A manifestation can usually occur with a very simple prayer of inviting the presence of the Holy Spirit and the laying of hands on the recipient. Nothing happened! We could see the frustration in Tim as well. He almost expected a manifestation just for proof of all the hardship that was going on in his life.

There didn't appear to be any spiritual attachments with Tim at all. Tim had a lot of bad things happen in his life: he lost his eyesight to a sickness and he had a crippling illness which forced him to walk with a cane. Sometimes bad things do happen to good people. Why? I don't know. But there is a fallen angel out there that seeks to destroy everything in creation.

At this point in ministry, Pastor Earl demonstrated the compassion of Jesus Christ and ministered to the individual's soul and inner wounds. I was so glad that God ordained the meeting with Pastor Earl to minister for this session. God knows what to do, and I believe He arranged the right deliverance team members for Tim. Tim received the truth about his situation. Tim's trials weren't due to demons or family curses; Tim simply had some hard times in life. It's not what Tim wanted to hear. It may happen that there aren't demonic manifestations during your prayer sessions. People would like to convince you what they're going through is demonic. They are seeking that magic "prayer," if you will. I have witnessed too many deliverance ministers start to call out demons in times like this when none are present. If there are no demons, that's that. The Holy Spirit is revealing the truth. Like Pastor Earl did with Tim, exercise the compassion of Jesus Christ with what the Holy Spirit is revealing to you about His creation in front of you. I never have a plan or an agenda, I simply show up to the prayer meeting and let Jesus do all the work. I find that prayer sessions run rather smoothly this way.

I know it's awkward to open a chapter on manifestations with the fact that you may not have a manifestation. A lot more people are avoiding their sanctification and instead are seeking the magic fix-all prayer. God wants us to become more like Him. He wants our soul to undergo a transformation. Sanctification and tribulations are something we walk out with Jesus, one-on-one. Be aware that a Christian can also invite a demon by giving it false credit for his hardships. Now the problem has become twofold: a demon comes in through "the devil made me do it" play card, and now the soul also must deal with the original problems of sin before the demon entered. "The devil made me do it" is a dangerous road to go down. A lot of Christians are using this approach to avoid their walk in sanctification. Spiritual direction is beneficial at this point in ministry. Call out the situation for what it is and keep the soul on the path of sanctification. Remember, they need to pick up their mat and walk. If the battle truly requires someone to come alongside, then proceed with deliverance ministry.

In the following sections, I am going to cover the basic forms of manifestations that may occur during a prayer session. Again, discernment is critical should any manifestation arise. Demons do not like to be found out. They would prefer to hide. Whenever a manifestation occurs, quietly and calmly bind the spirit in the name of Jesus Christ. The Holy Spirit is calm and orderly while demons like chaos. No yelling. If the demon is talking, bind it to shut up in the name of Jesus. Don't talk to it.

Eye Manifestations

The eyes are the window to the soul. When we do deliverance ministry, the objective is to have the person completely calm as we pray for him. A calm way to start ministry is by laying hands on the prayer recipient and inviting the Holy Spirit to manifest His presence. The Holy Spirit operates in calmness, not in chaos. If a spirit is present, it will be disturbed by the manifesting Holy Spirit. When the prayer recipient is relaxed and his eyes are closed, you may see eye movements underneath his eyelids.

When you see this happening, calmly ask the person to open his eyes and have him look at you. A spirit never wants to make its presence known. The spirit won't disturb the individual receiving prayer, but it will manifest around the eyes to take a look at what is going on. The spirit will try to keep the eyelids closed to avoid detection from the ministry team.

When you think you see this, or you are discerning with your body a manifestation is occurring, ask the person receiving prayer to open his eyes. Someone on the ministry team should then visually check the eyes to make sure it is still the same person looking back at you. It's not uncommon to have a demonic spirit glaring back at you through the eyes when this occurs. It may be a subtle difference, or it may be a significant difference, as though it is something else staring back at you through his borrowed eyes. Usually the manifestations are angry glaring eyes, or they are eyes petrified with fear. Very low-level grunt demons will manifest fearful eye glares. They know at this point they're prisoners of war. It's common for the eyes to be glossy and darker looking than usual. The demonic spirit is trying to avoid detection. If you're not sure if you're seeing the human soul or a demon, read Revelation 20 or Colossians 2:14-15 quietly and calmly, and you'll see the spirit react to the Scripture. If an evil spirit responds vocally to you, bind it to silence in the name of Jesus.

During a prayer session, there may be times when you examine the recipient's eyes and see an evil spirit looking back at you. A person may also faint when you look into his eyes and see a spirit. The spirit triggered the person to pass out. The demonic don't like their presence revealed because they know the prayer team will expel them.

When you detect a spirit looking back at you through the prayer receiver's eyes, bind the spirit immediately. Have the person keep his eyes open. Have someone watch the eyes as you pray. If a person faints, call the person by name to bring him back. Do not speak with the spirit. I calmly and gently ask for the person by his name to come up. You may have to do this several times as he wakes up and returns to his normal state.

It's common for the eyes to change appearance as if a different person is in the body, but with the same eyes. Many times the eyes look glassy during these manifestations. The spirit may also start speaking when this happens. Bind the spirit to silence. Continue with the deliverance prayer to liberate the soul and expel the spirit.

It's not uncommon either for a person to lie down on the floor, speak gibberish, and appear to have mentally checked out. This could also be a sign of dissociation. Just work in the prophetic with the Holy Spirit and lay hands on the person and cast out the spirits. Use discernment to determine if the person is experiencing a demonic manifestation or he is dissociating. Prayer ministers must be capable of true spiritual discernment and know the difference between manifesting demons and switching human parts.

Make sure you are not trying to cast out a dissociated human part. You will discern this because your body will not sense a demon with a dissociated human part, and yet your eyes will think they see a demon. This can be a bit tricky. In any case, stop the deliverance prayer and help the Christian core identity switch back in.

Be aware that eyes making circular motions are usually indicative of satanic ritual abuse programming. If the person is unresponsive when this is happening, there is a good chance you are dealing with occult programming and dissociation. The eye circles are a means of summoning witchcraft. Bind the witchcraft and ask the person, by his name, to come up. Cease deliverance prayer immediately.

On occasion, I have witnessed eyeballs roll backward. Use your discernment to sense the demonic manifestation. Do not use your physical eyes. Why? Because this could be a human part, from severe childhood trauma, that is in bondage to a demon. It may be a sign of either demonic possession or severe trauma. Either way, find a ministry team that can discern and deal with the unresolved issues. Stop the deliverance ministry and seek a prayer team that understands the difference between DID and demons. In outreaches where I have ministered to yoga masters and the Holy Spirit encountered them, their eyeballs would roll back and they would manifest their demons.

Weeping Manifestations

Weepy eyes and crying are most commonly signs of the manifestation of the Holy Spirit. In the Gospel of John, the Holy Spirit is also called the Spirit of truth[1]. A soul may have opened unwanted doors through diseased attitudes and ungodly belief systems. The words of condemnation may have systemically permeated the soul, but the Holy Spirit saturates the soul in truth. Truth sets the captive free from demonic strongholds. The prayer recipient will feel gentleness and peace as the Holy Spirit sets the soul free. You must exercise discernment, too, when the Holy Spirit is ministering so your team can be silent and let the Spirit of truth do all the work. Some ministers tend to talk too much during this deliverance manifestation. When I feel the presence of the Holy Spirit overshadowing the brokenhearted, I let the Holy Spirit do all the work. This means I pray silently as the Holy Spirit over shadows the heart and soul of the one it is healing.

The weeping and the healing presence of the Holy Spirit are the most common manifestations you will see in deliverance ministry. The most powerful deliverances come in the form of prayers and tears. The heart and soul releases repentance and the Holy Spirit heals wounds and lies with the power of forgiveness.

1 John 16:13

Be aware, too, that not all weeping is of the Holy Spirit. Spirits of grief or very low-level demonic spirits may start crying to deceive you. Some very low spirits may manifest, crying and attempting to plea bargain with you not to cast them out. They will even start pointing out the spirits who were involved in the torment of the individual, which, by the way, is tactical information that other spirits are present. Bind the weak spirit to the spirits it identified and continue to cast out this spirit.

Discernment is critical in this ministry. Discernment checks and balances with the ministry team are necessary. That's why working with a team of two is important—you need to discern what you see (physical, prophetic, and visions from God), feel (discernment), and hear (locutions) as being spiritual or physical.

When a person is wailing out loud and being distracting, it may be a spirit. Bind the spirit and order it to silence. Some spirits can be extremely loud when they're at the end of their tormenting rope. The spirit doesn't want to leave so it is as distracting as possible.

I mentioned earlier that my wife and I minister at a large pagan festival called Burning Man, held in Nevada, in the last week of August. Burning Man always builds a temple where people go once a year to release their pain. Lisa and I will minister in the temple where the souls are hurting and bring encounters with God. One year the temple was filled with spirits of death. Burning Man attendees will put up pictures and notes to people they lost in their life that year. There is typically darkness in these temples because it is essentially a pagan environment. For this particular year, the spiritual presence was death and grieving.

On this particular Burning Man outreach, while in the temple, we encountered one woman who was just wailing out loud in pain. I approached her to minister to her grieving but heard the Holy Spirit tell me to stop. Lisa got the same message at that moment. We discerned the woman had a spirit of grief. This spirit of grief was just cursing everyone that came by her with grief. It was like it was feeding off the grievances of others, and that was its hunting ground. We sat and observed this person for some time. Many who were grieving did what they came to do—release their pain and leave, but this woman just stayed in the temple area grieving with whoever would come her way. Lisa and I could feel the demonic presence as she moved out of our line of sight. When she was coming our way again, we could feel the demon of grief that was attaching to people. Lisa and I watched this woman as she talked with people and created these spiritual attachments with them. When you witness events like these, there is no rhyme or reason as to why the demon is doing this, other than it came to a spot where it knew it could draw energy from other people grieving.

Coughing Manifestations and Expelling Spirits

During prayers of liberation, the prayer recipient may start coughing as a spirit is leaving. Too many deliverance ministers rely on the coughing as a sign of a demon being cast out. Demons don't always leave the afflicted through coughing! Some deliverance ministers even instruct prayer recipients to cough after certain lines of prayer. Do not rely on this in your ministry and let your prayers become methodology. Satan will outflank you. There is no set process (of liberation prayers) for expelling demons. It is all up to the person wanting to be set free and the ministry of Jesus Christ. Demons leave because of our authority.

When we turn Jesus's ministry into a method and assume we know how to do things, we are operating in pride. Having a prayer recipient cough at the conclusion of a prayer in anticipation of expelling a demon is methodology. Leading a person through repentance prayer and then instructing him to cough is not deliverance ministry.

When you are praying for liberation and the spirit moves up out of the chest area and into the esophagus, the spirit might come out through coughing. Smaller spirits may be coughed out, and the bigger spirits may leave in a different manner. Just follow with what the Holy Spirit is doing in the prayer session. Again, God is God, and He doesn't owe you an explanation or a plan of what He is doing. The minister's job is just to stay in step with the will of the heavenly Father.

One of the disturbing things I have witnessed in deliverance sessions is that people know what deliverance looks like or they are obsessed with being delivered. During ministry, these individuals behave like a spirit is coming up through coughing. One person I worked with, Steve, was so obsessed with deliverance and being delivered that I could make stuff up and he would go through the coughing motions. I was mentoring a young woman, Katie, in deliverance while I was working with Steve. I leaned over to Katie and told her in a whisper to bind Daffy Duck. Katie whispered to bind Daffy Duck. All that Steve had to hear was that Katie bound a spirit. Steve started retching and coughing like crazy as he believed he was expelling a demon. We never told him that we bound Daffy Duck. Later we found out that Steve was sent to our prayer meetings as a distraction by the occult. There were occurrences when I believed I saw the occult astral project into him. With hindsight, I now believe that Steve was an SRA victim because of what the occult was able to do through him. Sadly, Steve would never accept the truth nor point his soul back to focus on Jesus. Steve was in bondage to a false prophecy spoken over him. It was a false calling, and he could never let go of that. It was this obsession over false prophecy which also led me to believe that Steve was an SRA survivor.

Again, if anyone presents a coughing methodology of Jesus's ministry to you, you'd better run in the opposite direction. One of the craziest situations I have ever seen with this involved a woman named Kelly. I and another counseling minister, named Jackie, was working with Kelly, who thought she was a UFO abductee. Ironically, Kelly was also Christian, and she mixed her New Age religion with Christianity frequently. The sad part was it wasn't just Kelly who did this. Kelly introduced me to the world of deliverance ministries that mix Jesus's ministry with that of the New Age.

When Kelly came in for counseling, she presented herself as the leading expert on UFO abductions and astral projection. The more Kelly divulged, the more I began to understand that Kelly was an SRA survivor with dissociative identity disorder. Kelly didn't want to listen to me. Kelly insisted that the voices she was hearing were galactic angels and reptilian species trying to morph her into the Nephilim. I instructed Kelly to stop her nightly deliverance sessions at once so Jackie and I could start working with the ritually abused parts. The alien abduction was a way of the occult to hide their human experiments agenda. I knew by listening and watching Kelly that she was DID. Kelly became irate and ignored my advice.

For the next counseling session, Kelly came in with a recording on her smartphone of the deliverance ministry I requested her to stop doing. On the phone was a New Age deliverance minister leading Kelly through the renouncement of galactic ruling angels and reptilian demons. Then the deliverance minister would order Kelly to cough and Kelly would retch up galactic ruling angels and reptile demons. There were about forty minutes of this on Kelly's phone as she renounced New Age spiritual and alien things. And she coughed about twenty times exactly at the phone minister's direction. Then Kelly told me, "See, I do need deliverance because they keep coming out of me!" At this point I realized that Kelly was not ready to receive healing. She'd heard the truth from our counseling sessions and she rejected it for occult deception.

My advice is always to be skeptical of what is going on in front of you and ask the Holy Spirit how to proceed. When the coughing up of spirits looks natural and is not acted out, then most likely the spirit is being expelled. Just always consult with the Holy Spirit as to what is going on. Keep in mind, too, that the strongman will kick out lower spirits to make it look like the strongman was expelled. Remember your discernment.

Growling and Screaming Demonic Manifestations

In most cases, demons will respond to liberation prayers, anointing oil, and the sprinkling of holy water with growling or screaming. Growling and hissing are common during prayer ministry. There have been times when I have worked with people over the phone, and both myself and the party I am working with heard audible disembodied growls. Sometimes a demon may be trying to evade detection during a deliverance session, so I will step away from my ministry team and read in a whisper, out of earshot, Revelation 20. The evading demon will respond with a growl or hissing. Then I know I am dealing with a demon during the prayer session. People with heart wounds may be harboring demonic oppression.

Bind the demons right away to silence. Many times the demons will continue to speak after being bound. Just bind them again. Never allow demons to distract a prayer service or deliverance session. If in a prayer group meeting or a church service, move the person to a quiet room. Then cast the spirits out.

I shared earlier in this book about Stacey, the woman involved in yoga, whose spirit manifested in church when the Holy Spirit manifested during the service. When I was brought over to silence the screaming manifestation, I bound the third eye and bound the demon to silence. At this point, the screaming demon had already disrupted the service. Pastors and clergy, do not allow screaming demons to disrupt group meetings or church services.

Deaf and Dumb Manifestations

Deaf and dumb spirits manifest in people who are perfectly capable of speaking. When a deaf and dumb spirit manifests, the afflicted soul may only be able to communicate with hand gestures. The demon may even force the lips to close against the person's will. Bind the spirit and authoritatively request that the person sit down, especially if he is flailing around. Deaf and dumb spirits usually have a lot of energy and can be troublesome. Command the spirit to release the person's voice.

Discernment again is critical here. Make sure you are sensing the presence of a demon and not a traumatized human part. With childhood abuse or ritual abuse, a human part may surface that can't talk in fear of being punished for speaking. In that case, you are dealing with a human part and not a demon!

By the way, many deliverance ministers will stop casting out a deaf and dumb demon because they think these will only come out through fasting and prayer (Mark 9). What Jesus was doing then, I believe, was correcting his pastoral staff, the apostles, for becoming doubtful about their spiritual authority. Jesus identified the spirit as a higher demon that required lots of prayer to be expelled. Jesus was defining the requirements of the saint to expel some of the nastier spirits. I don't believe the deaf and dumb spirit was the higher spirit in the demonic food chain here. The point is, whatever low-level demon is before you, pray and cast it out. Don't run home and fast for a week and then come back. Take instruction from Luke 10 that even the spirits submit to us in Jesus name.

Face Manifestations

As you lay hands on a person and pray, you may sense (by hearing God) that the spirit is working its way up and out of the prayer recipient. Spirits may work their way up from the reproductive, gastrointestinal, and respiratory organs, and sometimes, up through the throat and out of the mouth. This action can be indicative that the spirit is on its way out through the mouth. This point in deliverance can take time—from several minutes to hours to multiple sessions—for the unclean spirits to exit.

When my two older boys were in high school, they went with a youth pastor friend of mine to a Jesus Culture Conference. The worship at Jesus Culture is pretty powerful. The conferences are great for giving young people their first encounters with Jesus Christ. Some of the attendees get so moved spiritually that the Holy Spirit starts deliverance ministry inside them.

After the conference was over on a Saturday night, and the next day rolled over into Sunday morning, my middle son gave me a 1 a.m. wake-up call. When your kids are away and you receive a call at that early hour, you are in parental defense mode. What happened? Are you alright? Not the case here. My middle son started off the phone conversation with, "It's stuck!"

I asked him, "What's stuck?"

He said that he and his older brother were expelling a spirit of fear from a friend of theirs, and that the spirit was stuck on the face and wouldn't come off. I told my boys over the phone to bind the spirit and order it to release the face and order the spirit to go where the Holy Spirit told it to go. I was on the phone with them for about half an hour before their deliverance prayer session was successful. The spirit finally released the person's face and left. It took several repetitions of the boys standing in their authority to make the demon release the face and leave their friend. This prayer session was with my two oldest high-school-age sons, at the time, standing in their authority.

Don't be surprised if you spend time here ordering the spirit not to go back down into the person. Don't allow it to go back down. Bind it from going back and order it out completely. The spirit doesn't want to be expelled and as it is on its way out, it knows it is now a prisoner of war.

How do you know if the spirit is on the face? Sometimes the prayer recipient will tell you he can feel it on the face. Other times it may be in the throat on its way out, and spiritually holding on for its life and avoiding its expulsion. There may also be manifestations in the eyes looking back at you, and the facial muscles are all tense. There will be some noticeable sign on the person that the spirit is holding onto the face and doesn't want to leave.

As the spirit leaves the person, it may throw the person's head back as he exhales it out, or the spirit may scream on the way out. That's an indicator a spirit is leaving the afflicted soul of the person. Always consult the Holy Spirit on what is really happening. Remember, when there are manifestations, there can be, and usually are, more than one spirit. Be aware, too, that the strongman or root spirit will kick out little ones to make it look like it left.

Not all deliverances are the same. Don't always trust what you see or hear; listen to God for instructions. Spirits rely on lies and deception to derail the prayers of liberation. I commonly see demonic spirits do this manifestation on the face and lips when I am praying for deliverance ministry with former Jehovah Witnesses and Mormons. There is usually this behavior where the spirit clings onto the face and refuses to leave. Most of the time, the spirit is trying to stop the person from renouncing his sin. The spirit will lock up the lips. At this time, you pray,

> *"In the authority of Jesus Christ, I bind you. Loose the mouth and lips!"*

Internal Manifestations

It's not uncommon to be able to feel a spirit moving through a person's body physically. You may be laying hands on someone's back and feel a large mass move away from your hand. That's a spirit trying to get away from being expelled. Work in the prophetic and let the Holy Spirit guide your hands. The spirit may move the person away from you so you can't put your hand where the spirit is manifesting. Just stay with the spirit, bind it, and order it to go where the Holy Spirit tells it to go.

If the individual is exhibiting excruciating pain, like stabbing or electric shock, this can be a sign of programming and dissociation. Stop the deliverance prayer ministry and ask the Holy Spirit for revelation on what is going on. Human parts with dissociation will re-live the pain from their perpetrators. If you can't bind the pain to stop, it could very well be a dissociated part experiencing the pain.

Hand Manifestations

During deliverance prayer, you'll witness the hands do many strange things like clamping shut or shaking, or the oppressing spirit may try to defend itself using the person's hands. A common hand manifestation is a fist to punch a prayer team member. Bind the hands, using your spiritual authority, and order the spirit to release the hands. The hands will drop immediately. The hand manifestation with the fist is one good reason why you need to pray with your eyes open.

The spirit may also try to use the person's hands to harm them to bring the prayer session to an abrupt end. Spiritually bind the hands using prayer, anoint the hands with oil, and order the spirit to release the hands. The spirit may also use the hands for inappropriate finger gestures as well. Another common hand manifestation is with former occultists and psychics, who will manifest automatic handwriting during prayer liberation sessions.

Sometimes, when praying for healing, you may see hands tighten up and close. The clenching fists may be a sign of their harboring spirits of bitterness. The spirit of bitterness is a common manifestation when praying for physical healing in arthritis.

If a prayer bound hand breaks free and starts to pound the forehead, bind witchcraft and shut down the third eye. Ritual abuse parts will sometimes trigger and pound their forehead to summon more demons to the session. Use your discernment and make sure you are not dealing with a ritual abuse survivor. Ritual abuse survivors will also draw circles with their fingers, hands, and feet, to summon witchcraft. Be cautious of the occult programming. Even though the Christian host wants freedom, the occult-loyal parts inside them are cursing you. Shut down the deliverance ministry immediately if you stumble into ritual abuse. Ritual abuse prayer ministry requires experienced prayer ministers equipped for dissociative identity disorder.

Breathing and Tongue Gagging Manifestations

On occasion, a spirit may try to cause respiratory issues while you're praying. Don't be alarmed. Spirits may even try to make a person look like he is gagging on his tongue. Bind the spirit and order it to stop at once. Then command the spirit to release the breathing and the person's tongue.

If the person looks as if someone is gagging him or strangling him, be aware that this may be a ritual abuse survivor. A perpetrating part is inflicting harm through programming to silence the person or to stop him from seeking help. If you discern this is the case, stop the deliverance prayer session.

Incubus and Succubus Manifestations

This manifests as a spirit engaging in sexual activity with the person it is attached to. Keep in mind during prayer ministry that the incubus is the strongman. The strongman, sometimes called a *root spirit*, will kick out the other spirits making the prayer team think it has left too. The incubus spirit can be very deceptive to the prayer ministers.

The incubus is the male form of the spirit that typically visits women. The succubus is the female form of the spirit that manifests typically to men. These spirits tend to have their roots in witchcraft. They are most commonly transferred as a soul tie during sex. Be aware that a prayer minister can get slimed and experience an attack after the prayer session when he sleeps at night. Just bind the spirit and order it to leave. It's important that the prayer minister stay focused on Jesus and not have issues with sex and pornography, because sexual perversion sin will give the spirit a means of attachment. Ministry team members should not be dealing with sexual fantasies because this gives the incubus a toehold for torment.

When working with some women, they have had a difficult time in breaking off the attachment with the spirit because of the supernatural pleasure it brought them. However, it doesn't take long before the spirit torments with violence. Break the sexual, spiritual attachment off the afflicted soul immediately. If you are having difficulty with the prayer recipient breaking the attachment, boldly ask her if she is inviting it in. The spirit can easily reopen the door by offering intense sexual pleasure to the afflicted soul. Once the soul allows the attachment, the spirit becomes violent and difficult to expel. Some prayer recipients will yoyo with begging you to get rid of it and then go home and allow it to pleasure them. The soul must surrender to Jesus Christ and the heart must realign with the Holy Spirit. The soul must regain control of its free will and push out this externally stimulated desire from the incubus.

When working in prayer sessions and battling these spirits, it is not uncommon for ministers' private parts to be touched by spirits. Renounce it and bind the spirit, ordering it to not touch you. You usually notice when the spirits are touching your team by looking at the mortified expressions on prayer team members' faces.

If this activity continues, there may be spiritual attachments at home, or some activity the participant was involved in like ghost hunting, and he got slimed; but he won't share with you because he knows he shouldn't have been doing the activity. There is also the situation that if the spirit doesn't manifest during the day in the prayer session, the person could be an SRA victim, and this is what is called a night host identity. The spirit activity is occult programming being triggered by the night host.

Closing Thoughts on Spiritual Manifestations

Hopefully, this information will assist you in dealing with manifestations. I hope it sheds light on another reason why you don't start prayer sessions with binding all sorts of demons. You don't know what is truly going on until you hear the person tell his story, and you connect with God and hear from Him. There are lots of possibilities of what is going on with an individual. Just because he appears to be manifesting doesn't necessarily mean he is. Be the skeptic and discern if what is going on in front of you is demonic. Let the Holy Spirit guide you through the session. Let Him tell you if this is a session for prayers of liberation and expelling demons, for inner healing, or a time for someone to finally hear the truth and stop lying to himself. Remember, you can't trust what you're seeing you must develop your discernment!

CHAPTER 13

Authority and the Heavenly Realms

The hardest concept for the charismatic church to grasp is that we don't do any warring in the heavenly realms. Especially when it comes to spiritual authority and warfare, this topic is full of false doctrines I would like to address. You will find that many of these false teachings are heavily defended, even though there is no scriptural basis for telling us to war in the heavens.

If you get any message from this chapter, it will be that you are to stay out of the heavenly realms in warfare. If you are with a deliverance minister that is teaching you to go after beings in the second heaven or to attack regional spirits or principalities, you need to go face down to the floor, repent, ask the Lord for forgiveness, and leave this false instruction at once.

Man's Terrestrial Spiritual Dominion

Man's spiritual authority is terrestrial and does not extend into the heavenly realms. Jesus only gave us authority over the demonic spirits that roam the earth. Jesus reveals this in Scripture when He addresses the seventy disciples.

> *"Behold, I have given you authority to tread on serpents and scorpions, and over all the power of the enemy, and nothing will*

injure you."
- Luke 10:19

Jesus is telling His people that we have authority over the evil that slithers and crawls on the earth. When these demons attack us, we are to take authority over them. This prayer posture is called *low-level demonic deliverance.* They are called *low-level demons* because they are in the lowest of the ranks of the fallen angels bound to our earthly abode. We only engage the demonic when they attack us. We do not go hunting for them or go looking for a fight.

A lot of misconception and doctrine has been built around the false teaching that we war in the second heaven. There is a lot of contemporary Christian media and books out there that instruct Christians to sharpen their iron in the second heaven. This false teaching is dangerous. I believe the root cause of this teaching is the misinterpretation of Ephesians 6:12: "For our struggle is not against flesh and blood, but against the (heavenly) rulers, against the powers, against the world forces of this darkness, against the spiritual forces of wickedness in the heavenly places" (Ephesians 6:12).

This Scripture states that our earthly kingdom is at war with satanic angels in heavenly places, and we only have authority over this earthly kingdom. One of the books I taught for a deliverance seminar class identified these satanic angels as demons, but this grouping is of satanic angels with low-level demons is inaccurate. It leads people into believing they have authority in the heavens. Demons are not in heavenly places. They are roaming the earth. Evil angelic beings are waging war from the second heaven. Understand your spiritual covering and authority. It will keep you safe in warfare. In Ephesians 6:12, Paul is explicitly identifying a hierarchy of dark satanic angels and not demons.

Jesus never instructed us through Scripture to take authority or war in the heavens. If we look at the next verse, it begins with the word therefore. In the words of the late Derek Prince, "When you see a 'therefore', ask 'What's the therefore, there for.'"

> "Therefore, take up the full armor of God, so that you will be able to resist in the evil day, and having done everything, to

stand firm." -Ephesians 6:13

We are to take up the armor of God as a defensive measure. The only offensive weapon is the sword, which is the Word of God. We are not to flail it around. The Word of God is to be used in precision to strike against the enemy. God does not tell us to take up our swords and battle in the second heavens. Because of the war with the satanic angels in the second heaven, we are to put on our armor of God to protect us from evil. The satanic angels are warring and plotting over the earth. We need the armor of God to protect us from the warfare we encounter in this world because of these dark forces. God is our protection and our covering.

God and His Messengers

God is a mystery, and God is God. When we bring God into spiritual warfare through our petitioning prayer for help, there is no telling how He is going to end the battle. I have been in far too many battles where I have witnessed people petition for God's supernatural help and then at the same time ask for Him to send His angels into battle. What you are doing here is asking God for His help and then telling Him how to fight His battle. This position of praying is operating out of pride. When you are on the battlefield, you must operate in absolute humility. As prayer warriors, we must learn to die to ourselves and our human reasoning, and learn to live strictly by God's will. A friend of mine, Mark Neitz, says it like this, "You can't kill a dead man." That is true on the spiritual battlefield. We're human and we're completely fallible, but if we can, we must stay in imitation of Jesus and focus on operating in humility.

Many charismatic churches believe they can partner with angels. To some extent we can, but not in the manner popular in churches today. The way we partner with angels is through the "Our Father" prayer. We ask the Lord's kingdom to come and for His will to be done! You can sure bet you'll be partnering with angels in this operation. We will never know how we partnered until we go to heaven. This manner of freeing ourselves from resolving God's battles is a good protocol for spiritual warfare. I have seen some crazy things happen with angels. I saw an angel of judgment manifest in a possessed man in the city of San Francisco. I have felt and seen angels manifest physically during deliverance ministry. I have witnessed an invisible angel fly through a wall and drag a demoniac, lying face down on the floor, kicking and screaming, backward several inches, with her nails dug into the carpet. The angel took with it a spirit of rape. I have seen angels standing guard in my house. I just want to make it clear that I am not in unbelief about working with angels. I occasionally get to see them in their glory, and that's because of the grace of God. The fact of the matter is that all angels belong to God and God alone.

> *"The heavens are the heavens of the Lord, but the earth He has given to the sons of men"*
> *-Psalm 115:16*

The heavens belong to Jesus. We don't command angels. Remember that we are lower than angels.[2] When I am in an intense spiritual fight, I will petition in prayer for God to release His resources and I leave it at that. God is the general in this theater of warfare, and I let Him direct the battlefield. Angels belong to God, not us. Angels respond to God's voice only: "Bless the Lord, you His angels, mighty in strength, who perform His word, obeying the voice of His word!" (Psalm 103:20).

The biggest problem of partnering with angels is that you may connect with false angels of light. I remember Graham Cooke sharing a story at a conference some years back about a female deliverance minister who partnered with an angel in deliverance ministry. The minister over time became possessed by the spirit working with her. You always have to be on your toes in this ministry. The enemy is looking for every opportunity to take out a deliverance minister.

At this same conference, Graham Cooke had the same message about partnering with angels: Don't talk with them. One young lady got her halo bent out of shape in the audience when she heard that and shouted out to Graham, "That's not true!"

Usually, deliverance ministers and intercessors are at risk of being seduced into this. Just remember Psalm 115:16—heaven belongs to the

---

2 Hebrews 2:9

Lord! We stay out of heavenly places until we go on to glory or God mystically gives us a revelation of heaven, like He did with the apostle Paul. This means we don't bind Satan, regional spirits, or principalities in heavenly places. These are critical heavenly warfare protocols to take to heart here. Man doesn't have the authority to command, bind, or judge angels. God gave us the authority to bind low-level (angels) demons that are roaming the earth, but our authority does not extend in any way beyond this.

The Second Heaven

We have established now that the high-ranking, ruling satanic angels, and powers are in the second heaven. The highest ruling angel in the second heaven is the one with the title of Satan. When God cast Satan out of the third heaven for the failed rebellion, Satan took his ruling angels with him and set up his dominion in the second heaven.

What is the second heaven? In 2 Corinthians 12:2, Paul reveals to us he visited the third heaven, where God resides without the rebelling angels. Ephesians 6:12 tells us that the rebelling satanic hierarchy is in heavenly places. Satan wants to be God, so he has his own version of heaven, the second heaven. I recall listening to an old Derek Prince sermon when he described it along the lines of, "If there is a third heaven where the God most high resides, then by logic there must be a second heaven."[1]

Human reasoning likes to think in linear ways, and there is a theory that the first heaven is our universe, the second heaven is a little bit farther out, and the third heaven is beyond that. This linear model I believe to be inaccurate. Our minds can't comprehend the geometry and location of the heavens. These are spiritual realms and are most likely void of geometry and space, as we understand it. The second heaven is a spiritual realm and Satan is its ruler.

---

1 Derek Prince, Spiritual Warfare in Heavens and Earth.

The Spiritual Protocols of Jude 8-10

You have more than likely heard people pray and bind Satan and principalities in their prayers. This prayer practice is another false teaching in the church that is running rampant and is dangerous. Remember, we don't have authority over angelic beings. We are lesser than the angels.

> *"But we do see Him who was made for a little while lower than the angels, namely, Jesus, because of the suffering of death crowned with glory and honor, so that by the grace of God He might taste death for everyone."*
> *-Hebrews 2:9*

One of the ministry outreaches the Holy Spirit asked me to do was at the Berkeley Pagan Festival. The Sunday before the weekend of the outreach, my team was prayed over at a church service. The pastor who led the prayer started binding Satan and principalities. As the pastor prayed over us, I entered into mental prayer with Jesus and repented and asked for forgiveness of this prayer that was intended to pick a fight with the demonic. I asked for peace for the next weekend as my team prepared spiritually to go to the event and do the Father's will. We were going there in peace—not for a fight! Why did I pray to cancel the prayer? Because the pastor went outside his dominion with his prayers and was picking a fight in the heavenly realms, namely the second heaven. We can't bind Satan and his angels. Always seek answers in Scripture, fast, and use mental prayer with the Holy Spirit. When in doubt, lean on the side of humility when it comes to angelic realms. We don't have authority over the dark angels. God never revoked their positions or hierarchy. The Scriptures provide protocols in the book of Jude for dealing with angelic majesties, giving the example of the archangel Michael arguing with Satan over the body of Moses. Look at how the high-ranking archangel Michael, the key angelic figure in God's heavenly war, deals with Satan, our enemy.

> *Yet in the same way these men, also by dreaming, defile the flesh, and reject authority, and revile angelic majesties (evil dignities - KJV). But Michael the archangel, when he disputed with the devil and argued about the body of Moses, did not dare pronounce against him a railing judgment, but said, 'The Lord rebuke you!' But these men revile the things which they do not*

understand; and the things which they know by instinct, like
unreasoning animals, by these things they are destroyed.
-Jude 8-10

Verse 8 tells us not to reject authority and not to revile angelic majesties. Who are the angelic majesties? Satan and all the other choirs of angels called out in Ephesians 6:12. These are the ranks of the angelic majesties. In the Greek, they're referred to as cosmic or celestial beings.

Michael did not speak a slanderous word of judgment against Satan, but said, "The Lord rebuke you!" Michael is our angelic leader in spiritual warfare, demonstrating how God wants us to deal with Satan. We are not to revile the celestial beings. We do not bind them or slander them. We don't have the authority. And apparently through Scripture, neither do the high-ranking angels. There is another demonstration of this protocol found in Zechariah: "Then he showed me Joshua the high priest standing before the angel of the Lord, and Satan standing at his right hand to accuse him. The Lord said to Satan, 'The Lord rebuke you, Satan! Indeed, the Lord who has chosen Jerusalem rebuke you! Is this not a brand plucked from the fire?' Now Joshua was clothed with filthy garments and standing before the angel" (Zechariah 3).

When do we use the Jude 8-10 protocol in deliverance ministry? Hardly ever! This protocol comes into play during warfare if you are involved in battles against the occult or doing special prayer ministry for satanic ritual abuse survivors.

Petitioning Warfare with a Regional Spirit

Around two years ago I had an interesting spiritual warfare case. Connie, from Africa, contacted me for deliverance ministry. Her job had her traveling back and forth between Africa and California. She initially contacted me because she was levitating in her bed at night. After the phone assessment, I decided to bring her into the office for Anna, who was assisting me in ministry, and myself, to hear more about what was going on with her. Before you do any form of ministry, sit down and listen to the person to determine what is going on. Connie explained to us that she was the first Christian in her family. As a child, she had been taken quite a bit to local witch doctors for her maladies. As an adult, Connie gave her life to Jesus and sought the baptism of the Holy Spirit. Not long after her baptism with the Holy Spirit, Connie started suffering from severe demonic oppression.

As Connie's story unfolded, she also told us about how deliverance ministers in her village were struck down dead right after praying for her. The smiting of the ministers was interesting. Demons don't strike down deliverance ministers. Connie's story was pointing to something higher up on the satanic angel food chain. I asked Jesus for more revelation on Connie and her history. She spoke with us for a good hour, and finally Connie provided the pieces to the puzzle that were missing.

Connie said since she was the first Christian in her family, being delivered from this would have huge spiritual implications in her village back home. Connie's father was both the governing and spiritual leader for their region. With this revelation in the story, the battle was leaning toward regional spirits. What are these? Satanic angels! This information was the piece to the puzzle that explained the horrible death of the deliverance ministers. Satan has no sympathy for ignorance. He struck down these deliverance ministers for stepping out from underneath their covering. Jesus gave us the revelation here on how the battle needed to proceed. At this point, I also had peace that the Father would allow me into this battle. Always be released into battle, never run into a fight with spirits. This kind of battle is a petitioning prayer for Jesus, who has authority in all the heavenly places, to shut down the assignments and the witchcraft. I started the prayer session by opening with Scripture and reading Jude 8-10 as a prayer. It was very calm and very peaceful. In these petitioning prayers, you do not tell Jesus how to carry out the fight. You simply ask Jesus to shut down what is coming from the dark heavenly places.

The only warfare prayer we did was binding any low-level demonic spirits involved from calling out to higher spirits. We shut down the communication and assignments that we had terrestrial authority over.

The result was that after two prayer sessions, the levitation stopped at night. The ministry was all done through petitioning prayer to Jesus, and neither Anna or I, were struck down or had assignments against us.

Spiritual Warfare and Principalities

The number one rule of spiritual warfare is not to revile or battle angelic majesties. In my years of ministry, every person that has come to me claiming to be under the attack of a principality wasn't. I have heard people in church ignorantly bind principalities and claim they saw them manifest in a church service. I have also worked with an individual who claimed her family was under the curse of a principality that dated all the way back to the days of Babylon. This woman had a fantastic and colorful story, but two things didn't add up: why she was in great health and why the warfare on her was so trivial. And the big question I always ask is: why were the principalities even remotely interested in this individual? Remember, principalities have low-level angelic foot soldiers called demons to do this sort of thing. Always be the biggest skeptic and tear apart their story.

We are given a clear example in the book of Daniel about an attack by the Prince of Persia, a principality. The satanic angel was not battling Daniel, it was battling God's angels. The reason the principality was even in the picture is that there was about to be a regional change, prophesied by God: the Israelites were to be set free from their bondage in Babylon. Daniel read about God's prophecy in the Scriptures and realized it was about to be fulfilled. Daniel, being an exemplary man of God, entered into fasting and prayers of supplication. He prayed into the heavenly Father's will, praying for God's will to be done. He wasn't battling a principality. God sent angels unbeknownst to Daniel. The spiritual warfare was the unseen result of Daniel's prayer and obedience to God. When the warfare ended, the angel Gabriel informed Daniel of the battle that took place in the spiritual realms. The battles in the heavenly places belong to Jesus. The lead warrior is Michael the archangel. Michael, who also is a prince, deals with the principalities, not us. We are to stay out of the heavenly battles.

Whenever someone in your church claims to be fighting in the heavens and engaging regional spirits and principalities, he is reviling angelic majesties. There are huge consequences to this ignorance in spiritual warfare protocol. In his book, *Unnecessary Casualties of War*, John Paul

Jackson documents churches that received congregation-wide curses of cancer and miscarriages from overstepping their spiritual authority.

The Occult and Satanic Angels

Whenever your ministry gets cases involving satanic rituals and blood sacrifices, you have stepped into the occult. Satanic angels of the occult desire men to worship them. Great care, consideration, and respect must be given to this spiritual darkness that is beyond human reasoning. The majority of the body of Christ in the church has never really seen true evil, which can be a good thing, but from the spiritual warfare perspective, this can get a minister into lots of trouble. Many deliverance ministers have seen the darkness of the enemy, but most haven't seen the depths of evil the occult is capable of afflicting people with. Never run into a battle with the occult. Always ask God to be released into these high-level spiritual fights. If God says no, then stay out of the fight! God is your covering in battle.

I have worked with numerous people and pastors who have gotten spiritually attacked because they stepped outside their dominion and engaged in warfare against the occult. One pastor I know merely went out to a house that had started having demonic activity, so the father of the home requested for the house to be blessed. The spiritual activity started when the man's son thought it would be fun to get drunk and high in the family pool house while his parents were away on vacation. One of the kids had a copy of Anton LaVey's satanic bible on him, and he decided to read from it for some laughs and giggles. The readings invited more guests to the party. A demonic spirit occupied the pool house after the party, and all the kids involved became demonically oppressed. It wasn't so much that the kids just read from the book, they enacted rituals. They were too high to remember what they did, but it was sufficient to bring something nasty into our reality. The kids knew right away something bad happened, and it was no longer partying fun and games. From that moment after, shadow apparitions were appearing in both the pool house and the family home on the property.

Thankfully, this family had a pastor who stood in the victory of the cross; however, he used the wrong spiritual warfare protocols. The pastor ended up getting cursed in the pool house. My ministry calls this form of instant demonic oppression "getting spiritually slimed." The pastor immediately experienced an inexplicable dark oppression that attached to him, and he couldn't shake it. This mystical experience was unnerving for him because he didn't know that the demonic could attach in such a way. He had thought he was unshakeable because of his conventional warfare prayer approaches. The pastor sought out M16 Ministries and we cleaned him up. And the pastor received an education in cleaning up defiled locations.

Another church I work in close collaboration with called me about a black, six-winged angel with red eyes (the red eyes are usually indicative of a ritual spirit) that was seen at night walking the halls of the house of one his church members. The pastor, a close friend of mine, called me for my thoughts. I told him the reason the satanic angel was there was because someone had performed a blood ritual to invite the spirit. My friend thanked me for the information and then told me that God revealed to him that the family grandmother in the house was practicing Santa Muerte.[2] I gave my friend some tools on helping cleanse the home. A few days later the dark angel was gone.

The pastor and the prayer team met with the grandmother and had her renounce and revoke her dark rituals. The pastor in this situation didn't get spiritually slimed. He took a Holy Spirit pause, spoke with God, and then was released into the fight. The outcome of the battle was victorious and the dark angel has never been seen again in the house.

The message here is to avoid taking on the occult alone. Find teams that are seasoned in these battles. Your favorite conference speaker, whose books line your library, is not usually your best bet in this fight. Remember, he (or she) is a public figure and he is not in the trenches of battle.

---

2 Nuestra Señora de la Santa Muerte (Spanish for Our Lady of the Holy Death) or, colloquially, Santa Muerte (Holy Death), is a female deity (or folk saint depending on school of thought) Mexican folk religion.

SRA Survivors and Occult Battles in the Heavens

Another instance where you can encounter satanic angels in warfare is when working with satanic ritual abuse (SRA) survivors. As I mentioned before, ritual abuse is a special prayer ministry that is different from deliverance ministry. Here you must have dead-on discernment and have the ability to discern between demons, angels, human identities, and astral-projecting witchcraft. These prayer sessions are intense, and one-on-one prayer ministry can go on for years to help heal the survivor. A minister must understand the different styles of warfare and protocols and know when to implement them. During these battles, you will encounter biblical deities, Baal, Moloch, and satanic and Luciferian angels.

People who minister to SRA survivors must have a clear-cut understanding of the power of the occult. Attacks on the ministry can go on for years as you minister to one individual. In my ministry, we have several survivors we minister to, so it compounds the spiritual attacks that can and do occur. You live in a warzone in this ministry. We keep our sanity through all this because we fear God and not the enemy. No matter how intense the warfare may get, we always see the glory of God. If you encounter an SRA survivor needing help, seek out the ministries that already work in these areas. At the time of this writing, there are only a handful. Do not tackle this on your own or from the perspective of deliverance.

Some ministries use an approach of partnering with angels to bring healing to SRA survivors. Again, this is dangerous, especially when SRA deals with angels masquerading as a false Jesus and false angels of light. Jesus alone can use angels in ministry. Because of the level of deceit from the occult, never use the partnering with angels approach to ministry.

In SRA ministry prayer, let Jesus and the Holy Spirit do all the work and all the thinking. Many people have a hard time with this, but this is the basis of deep faith in spiritual warfare—that Jesus can handle everything. When you send in your angels, you are overstepping your spiritual authority and boundaries. I seriously doubt it is your angels responding to you.

Battling in the Heavenly Realms

Not all battles are low-level demonic deliverance prayer sessions. In deliverance ministry, you most likely won't encounter satanic angels. If you discern you are dealing with something angelic, switch to petitioning prayer to Jesus.

Petitioning Prayer

It is Jesus alone we pray to and petition. Jesus who was God incarnate. Jesus, who was born by a virgin birth. Jesus who came into this world as a man, not under the curse of the original sin. Jesus, who led a sinless, holy life. Jesus who was the only true blood sacrifice for man's sins. Jesus who died on the cross, and rose from the grave in three days. Jesus, who is the only way to the Father in heaven. It is this Jesus alone we pray to and petition. Jesus, the heavens belong to you alone.

Jesus, if there is any warfare coming from the heavenly places, we ask that you shut this down. Please protect us and cover us. Please cancel any assignments against us. Protect and cover us, our ministries, our properties, and our families.

Anything under our dominion, we bind and forbid from calling out to higher beings. We bind witchcraft and bind the demonic from their sources of power. Jesus, we ask for your revelation, your covering, and your protection.

The only time a deliverance minister should have to use this prayer is if he finds himself working with a former occult member and not an occult ritual survivor. In this event, the deliverance minister needs to seek a legitimate exorcist for assistance.

CHAPTER 14

The Ministry of Exorcism

E xorcism is the most controversial, confused, dangerous, and feared ministry in Christianity. As Christians, we don't have a firm understanding of what this ministry is all about. Many charismatic Christians use the words deliverance and exorcism interchangeably. A few years ago I was interviewed for a documentary on exorcists by Dr Jerry Johnston of Crossroads Christian Communication in Canada. What surprised me about the interview was that all the questions were about low-level demonic deliverance ministry. This filming session led me to believe the documentary producer didn't have a clear understanding of the difference between the ministries. I am not knocking Dr Johnston, I just think this interview was reflective of how very little many Christians understand about the ministry of exorcism.

The fact of the matter is that deliverance and exorcism are not one and the same. The objective of exorcism is to provide pastoral care to the soul of an individual under high-level spiritual attack. Souls that are under severe oppression and attack by

the occult,

spiritual attachment of demonic spirits,

satanic angelic beings, or

are demonically possessed

will require the pastoral direction of a minister of exorcism.

The late Father Gabrielle Amorth, who was the leading spiritual director of exorcism for the Roman Catholic Church, made the distinction between the ministries of deliverance and exorcism in his book, *An Exorcist Tells His Story*. He wrote:

> *"These signs will accompany those who believe: in my name they will cast out demons" (Mark 16:17). This power, which Jesus granted to all those who believed in him, is still fully effective. It is general power, based on prayer and faith. It can be exercised by individuals and by communities. It is always available and does not require special authorization. However, we must make it clear that in this case we are talking about the prayers of deliverance, not of exorcisms.* [3]

Fr Amorth was alluding to the distinct differences between the ministries of deliverance and exorcism. The ministry of deliverance is the expelling of demons through the spiritual authority and the faith of the believer. I defined this earlier in this book as *low-level demonic deliverance*. When the seventy disciples returned (Luke 10:17) and reported to Jesus that even the demons submitted to His name, they were operating as ministers of deliverance. Deliverance ministry is effective when done by all believers who stand in their authority against demons.

But something curious happened when the disciples—minus Peter, James, and John—were unable to cast the demons of a possessed boy (Mark 9). The father of the boy was perplexed as well and thought his son couldn't be delivered from these demons. He had just witnessed Jesus's disciples fail at expelling these spirits. The boy's father then doubtfully asked Jesus if He could cast them out. Jesus rebuked the father for his unbelief. Then in a single command, Jesus said, "You deaf and dumb spirit, I command you out of him, and never return" (Mark 9:25). The evil spirits left the boy as Jesus commanded.

In this account, the disciples who were expelling the demons were mystified as to why they had failed. This humiliation was unexpected, and after the incident, the disciples met with Jesus and asked Him why they couldn't cast the demons out. "When He came into the house, His

---

3 Fr Gabriele Amorth, *An Exorcist Tells His Story* (San Francisco, Ignatius Press, 1999), 43.

disciples began questioning Him privately, 'Why could we not drive it out?' And He said to them, 'This kind cannot come out by anything but prayer'" (Mark 9:28-29).

This outcome is not the same as with the seventy disciples (Luke 10), when Jesus's twelve disciples had successfully cleansed souls of demoniacs. The situation was clearly an embarrassment to the disciples. What was different? Jesus indicated there was something different about this demoniac that the disciples had not encountered before. Low-level demonic deliverance, which the disciples were well equipped at ministering, was ineffective in this spiritual battle. In the context of the Scripture, it appears that Jesus was subtly upset at his apostles for not having the level of faith to expels these demons. Jesus also commented that this kind only came out with prayer. This inclusion of prayer alludes to a deeper level of spiritual warfare than the apostles were accustomed to.

In low-level demonic deliverance, the believer stands in his spiritual authority and commands the demon to leave. Jesus gave us the terrestrial dominion to expel the spirits on our own. The prayer stance is one of the believer standing directly against the demonic spirit (i.e. deliverance ministry). But if the spirits the disciples were dealing with could only come out through prayer (Mark 9:29), then the prayer warrior also needed to petition Jesus for His assistance in the expulsion. This context of Scripture suggests there are higher-level spirits that don't respond to deliverance ministry.

Jesus presented a higher-level of spiritual warfare which requires petitioning prayer for the liberation of a severely oppressed or possessed soul—what we now call the *ministry of exorcism.*

Exorcism

From a historical standpoint, let's take a look at the ministry of exorcism through the church's history. Exorcism is predominately considered to be a Roman Catholic ministry. To present the origins of exorcism ministry, I am going to rely on my notes from the 2012 Southern California Renewal Communities (SCRC) Roman Catholic Conference on Exorcism from Chicago archdiocese exorcist Father Jeff Grob. Fr Grob drew the roots of exorcism ministry from the gospels of Matthew (3:14-15; 10:1) and Luke (9:1). Through these Scriptures, an early church father in Africa, Tertullian, preached that any Christian could cast out demons. Special charisms (spiritual gifts from the Holy Spirit) were given to anyone who was baptized in Christ.

In the AD 300s, the Roman Catholic Church formed the Order of Exorcists. This activity was the grassroots effort by the Roman Catholic Church to deal with the rare cases of demonic possession. The demonically possessed received liberation through petitioning prayer to Jesus Christ. It wasn't long before abuse sprang up and charlatans were pretending to be exorcists. The Roman Catholic Church set up a system to stop the rampant abuse of exorcism. In AD 398, the Fourth Council of Carthage created Canon 7 for the ordination of exorcists. A canon is a law in the Roman Catholic Church. Canon 7 also referenced a book on exorcism to be given to the ordained ministers of the office. Fr Grob noted in his lecture that this original book of exorcism no longer exists, so no one knows what the original ritual of exorcism looked like.

The rite of exorcism was standardized in 1614. It has remained pretty much the same up until today, with only minimal changes. In the 1980s the Roman Catholic started relying heavily on psychology for demonic possession. The use of psychologists proved to be ineffective, and the church returned to the rite of exorcism for liberating the demonically possessed. In its current form, the rite of exorcism is strictly for casting out demons from souls that are possessed.

The rite of exorcism is the official ritual of the (Roman Catholic) Church in which a demon is ordered in the name of Christ to leave the body of a possessed person (see CCC 1673). While the ecclesiastical rite of exorcism contains many secondary parts (e.g. the litany of saints, the liturgy of the Word, the Lord's Prayer, etc.), its essence is the casting out of the demon. Nothing is ever asked of the demon; rather he is asked to depart in the name of the Redeemer. If an exorcism does not have a "casting out," it is not a true exorcism. [4]

---

4 Fr Jose Antonio Fortea, *Interview with an Exorcist* (*West Chester, Ascension Press, 2006), 93.

In the Roman Catholic Church, only an officially appointed priest can perform the rite of exorcism.

There are very serious and tough cases of satanic influence on certain individuals. This kind of effect is known as *possession*. Exorcism is the official prayer of the church which can be conducted only by the priest who has been officially chosen by a bishop in order to deliver the possessed. However, the right diagnosis should be made to identify whether it is a real case of satanic influence, disturbances, or the real presence of the Evil One in a certain individual.[5]

Exorcisms on the Lutheran Side of the Fence

Throughout history, the ministry of exorcism has belonged predominantly to the Roman Catholics. Exorcist Father Chad Ripperger once shared a story about a Protestant pastor who was trying to expel a demon out of a person who was levitating. The demon mocked the pastor and told him to get a Roman Catholic exorcist. The pastor did, the exorcist liberated the person, and he never levitated again. Here lies the dichotomy of theologies. I respect Fr Ripperger, his teaching, and his insight into spiritual warfare. Fr Ripperger claimed that only the Catholic Church could liberate this individual from demonic possession. To me, it makes no sense that God would only equip part of the body of Christ. It is my observation that the denominations under the Lutheran side have not fully embraced the victory of Christ in the way the Roman Catholics have. The Protestant pastor used low-level deliverance ministry techniques against the demon and failed, just like the apostles (Mark 9). What is fascinating about Fr Ripperger's story is that the demon was forced, under the authority of the Holy Spirit, to tell the pastor where to seek help in this situation. God is always in control in the deepest, darkest battles.

The big question here is, are there non-Roman Catholic exorcists? The answer to the question is yes. As I respond to this, keep in mind that we are all subjugated to church authority. I don't want to create a headache

---

5 Mons. Milivoj Bolobanic, *An Exorcist Speaks (Toronto, Ave Maria Centre for Peace, 2012),* 93.

I will have to deal with later by those who overzealously misread my words. Through the grace of God and His salvation, we all have dominion over the demonic and can carry out deliverance ministry (Luke 10).

Exorcism is not the next level of deliverance ministry. Some excellent deliverance ministers will never be exorcists, and God doesn't promote deliverance ministers into being exorcists. He needs those deliverance ministers where they are because there are so few good, legitimate ministries doing this. God selects His exorcists; no one volunteers for it. In the Roman Catholic Church, a bishop of the archdiocese of the region may select an exorcist. In the Protestant Church, the exorcist is raised up by the Holy Spirit. I refer to the selection process as "being drafted." I didn't even know I was on the path to becoming an exorcist. I made the assumption I was a deliverance minister because I was an Assembly of God church member. We don't have exorcists. It came as a shock to me, and I tried to refute it with the Holy Spirit. I told Him I wasn't a Catholic. It took some counseling from the Holy Spirit before I accepted my office of ministry. Isn't it interesting how we all default to the Catholic Church when it comes to exorcism?

I, and any other legitimate Protestant exorcist I have met, never saw this aspect of our life manifesting in this manner. The reason I believe this is so is for two reasons.

God likes stealth. You will not receive any glamorous recognition for being a Protestant exorcist. God needs His ministers to move freely and without recognition. In fact, you will receive more ridicule than accolades from the church. There is not a whole lot of respect for this pastoral office from the Protestant perspective, unless a church needs an exorcist, and then it becomes a different story. Roman Catholics are still highly skeptical of Protestant exorcists.

This is a very dangerous ministry, and you just don't enter into it because you want the thrill of battling demons. If you want to be an exorcist for notoriety or you're thrill seeking, then you need your head examined. Again, I direct all thrill seekers to go to Baja California and open cage dive with great white sharks. It would be a lot safer than this ministry. I, and others I know who are Holy Spirit-raised exorcists, have had their relationships, families, and marriages attacked. I have had my finances destroyed and have had weird car accidents. These were all orchestrated attacks by the enemy. I had one very heartbreaking incident early in my equipping when my dog was possessed and given violent brain seizures. When I took my dog to the vet to have him put down, and the vet inserted the syringe into my nearly lifeless friend, the dog violently shook and manifested as the demon left him. You don't enter into this ministry unless the Holy Spirit leads you into this. We still get attacked with oppressions, but we are under the spiritual covering of the Holy Spirit. That means our house is peaceful and the Holy Spirit dwells in it. We don't have demonic oppression lingering over our home. There is absolute peace in my home. If you look at paranormal television show hosts lifestyles, you will see their homes are full of demonic torment.

Demonic possession is rare, and so are the souls God calls into the ministry of exorcism. If I can do anything with these words here, they would be to steer you clear of this ministry. Probably not the words you wanted to read in a chapter about exorcism. I don't train people who come to me to learn about this ministry. The Holy Spirit will send me people to mentor, and I only train other exorcists in this capacity. I would like to give a word of advice here: Stay away from any exorcist training programs and orders of exorcism you find on the Internet. No matter how legit they look, there are only two schools of exorcism—the Holy Spirit and the Vatican.

Pastoral Care of the Soul

The role of the exorcist is to come alongside a severely afflicted or possessed soul and steer his focus back on Jesus Christ. The exorcist strengthens the soul of the afflicted through petitioning prayers to Jesus Christ for complete liberation. The demonically afflicted soul may be weak, but it must develop the strength to battle against the internal invaders. The prayers of the exorcist also inflict pain on the demonic as the internal struggle ensues. Again, this form of warfare differs from low-level demonic deliverance ministry. The minister must exercise the compassion of Jesus Christ on the afflicted soul, while also being vigilant and merciless against the forces of darkness. The Holy Spirit teaches you how to pray in this manner. The exorcist encourages and builds up faith in the soul as it works to expel the demonic captors.

The exorcist is also a counselor, assisting the soul in resolving traumatic and spiritual issues. Counseling the severely oppressed and possessed requires experience in spiritual direction. Many oppressed souls can't even cry out to God. The minister must deal with the person as a whole, including his walk in life, relationships, and basic everyday living. Severe oppression and demonic possession must many times be walked out because of old trauma or poor lifelong choices. Again, it's between God and the afflicted soul and however long healing takes. The goal of exorcism is a complete healing of the Christian core.

The Heart of God's Minister

As I stated before, God selects the exorcist. How and why He does this, I don't know. What I do understand is that He selects average people. We are normal human beings whose souls are broken and we are dealing with original sin like the rest of humanity. The exorcist has a profound love for Jesus Christ and His ways. The soul and heart of the exorcist are deeply seeking to imitate Jesus Christ. The matter of sanctification of his soul and the souls of others is a serious matter to the exorcist.

The minister is a representative of the kingdom of God and the human compassion of Jesus Christ. No matter how evil or vile the words or actions coming out of an oppressed or possessed person are, the minister continues to fight for the complete freedom of the soul. This ministry is not for the squeamish. In deliverance ministry, you deal with the soul and its sinful nature. In the ministry of exorcism, you deal with absolute evil and with the forces of darkness. Horrific things happen to children in the hands of the occult. That's if they survive the ritual. You will deal with children who were oppressed in their mother's womb and then buried alive with corpses to complete a ritual of possession. Only through the grace of the Holy Spirit do I believe I survive these sessions with my humanity intact.

The soul that is sitting in front of you in counseling will wonder if he's oppressed, possessed, or has a fractured soul from trauma. The exorcist must have the spiritual maturity in discernment to tell him what is going on with him. Rattling off spirits like a poorly trained deliverance minister will hurt the soul seeking help. I don't know how many times a person has sat in front of me in counseling and thought he was possessed because a charlatan deliverance minister told him he saw this demon or that demon on him. Demons do show up in sessions, and I will identify them when it happens, but not all sessions are demonic cases. Many people show up in my office because an ill-equipped deliverance minister told someone he had a demon. Many times a person has a fractured soul, or he has a really bad stronghold he needs to take responsibility for through his actions and daily life choices. An exorcist must provide the truth to the soul sitting in front of him during a ministry session. When the truth is presented, a spiritual direction must also be presented to assist the soul in getting back on the right track to Jesus Christ.

Finally, the exorcist must not seek recognition for the work of liberating souls. Even though we go through a great deal of internal oppression during spiritual warfare, oppression the average person may never fathom, we don't do any of the work on freeing the soul. The Lord Jesus Christ does all the work. The minister just comes alongside the soul in warfare to assist and give direction toward spiritual freedom. Keep in mind that the exorcist will be involved in multiple theaters of intense spiritual warfare. Early on when the Holy Spirit was training me, I only worked with one soul at a time in warfare. Now that the Holy Spirit has me at a more mature point in my ministry, I work with about eight to ten people in one form or another of spiritual liberation. All of these assignments are long term, and I work with people from months to years. As I mentioned, the warfare is intense, and it is beyond the scope of what church pastors will be able to assist you with in your interior prayer life. This complex intercession of dealing with multiple occult and demonic battles is what makes the ministry of exorcism unique. And on top of this, the exorcist must pray and deflect onslaughts of oppression directed at him. The exorcist must be of sound state of mind because of the level of oppression that attacks his thoughts. The exorcist always knows that victory comes through Jesus Christ, despite how run down and fatigued he may get during spiritual warfare. There are no books to teach this prayer practice. The Teacher teaches it through lots of contemplative prayers. When I enter into battle, it is the certainty of the indwelling triune God that protects me. I have seen the demonic fear the God inside me. I know it is because of my relationship with God and because of prayer and Holy Spirit meditation.

Protestant Style Exorcism

I will discuss the prayer concepts of exorcism from a non-Catholic Christian perspective. After all these centuries, there are still some unrepaired wounds on both sides of the fence after Martin Luther's actions. I know firsthand of some deep animosities between the Lutheran and the Catholic Church body. This division is not of God, and most people I know who harbor these irreconcilable differences haven't considered the notion that God doesn't like division among the mystical church body of Jesus Christ. I have had the pleasure of working with Catholics who understand that the body of Christ must unify for the end-time church to fulfill her objective.

As I present my approach to exorcism without the Rite of Exorcism, it is by no means to present a better way. What I am presenting is the concept of what exorcism looks like in the Protestant Church. I uphold the highest respect toward my Roman Catholic exorcist friends who have welcomed me as a colleague. Although I am still not allowed into the International Association of Exorcists, which is strictly for Roman Catholic clergy, I hope one day our denomination's ministry efforts will be recognized. There is so much we can share with each other regarding spiritual warfare and fellowship.

Let's examine some concepts of an exorcism. First of all, you will notice that there is no methodology to it. This session is not a ritual, this is a battle with the forces of darkness. God has built you up in previous battles, and you walk into the session with the certitude of victory through our Lord Jesus Christ. Whatever happens in the session is under the control and direction of the Holy Spirit. There is no way to prepare for these battles other than to show up and know full well in advance that Jesus is going to do something in the session. The only things I usually bring to these sessions are a Bible and anointing oil. I don't bring a theatrical crucifix or wear a collar. In our counseling office, there are various crucifixes on the walls. I bring myself and my ministry team, who have the temple of God inside them. Again, it's about character and who the ministry team is in Christ. If there are demons present, we will get comments or manifestations right away because of the presence we carry inside us.

I borrow a lot of concepts and theology from Roman Catholic Spanish mystics of the 1500s. Saint Teresa of Avila and Saint John of the Cross provided some great information on the spiritual makeup of the minister.

The minister must carry the presence of God within him. A Christian mystic is a soul that connects with God in his interior life. I am not talking about prophecy and visions. I am merely saying we can connect with the indwelling Jesus inside us. This feeling of the indwelling presence comes through having a relationship with the triune God. There are a lot of mystical experiences in an exorcism prayer session. It is the Father in heaven whom directs the prayer session.

An exorcist may or may not see the spirits in the physical, outside of the manifestations and indicators he may feel in his body. Again, the ministry is completely under the control of God. We see spiritual things under His grace and mercy alone. During some exorcisms I may fly completely blind and only feel sensations in my body of the demonic manifestations. These sensations may include:

pressure on the head,

sometimes a sudden migraine, which I am not prone to having.

I may feel pressure on my chest or

uneasiness in my stomach.

Over time, you learn to recognize what are signs of manifestations through your own body alarms. I never pay attention to what I am seeing in front of me. I always listen to Jesus and the Holy Spirit as they guide me in a session.

The exorcist must be mature in his interior prayer life to understand the words of knowledge and urges from the Holy Spirit that will come in during the session. By a word of knowledge, I mean I am getting tactical information that takes me one step ahead of a diabolic plan. Don't misconstrue a word of knowledge with calling out names of demons. That is a dangerous approach. If you're getting nothing in a session, then that is conclusive information. Be very aware of how the triune God speaks inside you. It's very sublime.

The exorcist must be the biggest skeptic. I have been called in to provide a second opinion to souls who had been misdiagnosed by very well-known deliverance ministers. This happens. We're human beings, and we're fallible. Far too many times a fractured soul was called out as a demon. And many times a fractured soul believes it is a demon, which is why we must use discernment and test the spirit.

Because of all the spiritual dynamics of spirits and fractured souls during a session, it is a good idea to establish the true identity of the Jesus you want present during your ministry session. I open a prayer session by establishing the true Jesus Christ with the following prayer:

> True Lord Jesus, born through your virgin mother, Mary; Jesus, who led a sinless, holy life. Jesus, you followed the will of your heavenly Father to the cross and were the only true sacrifice for mankind's sin. Jesus, you died on the cross and were resurrected from the grave through the power of the Holy Spirit. It is to you and you alone we speak to in this prayer session. Jesus, we ask you to push out all false representations of you in this session.

The session is opened in prayer like this because the occult will use false Jesus in their rituals. False Jesus can show up in your session as a demonic spirit pretending to be Jesus or as an occult fractured soul programmed to think it is Jesus. The false Jesus can and will cause havoc in your prayer sessions. It takes time and development of discernment to determine when this occurs in your session. True Jesus is the leader of the prayer team. He is present during the session, and false Jesus is a nasty diversion placed in the soul by the occult to interrupt ministry progress. Depending on the situation (i.e. if a person was a part of the occult but not a ritual abuse survivor, he allowed himself to be subjugated to demonic inhabitation), then false Jesus will be present as a dark spirit in a Messiah role. If the soul before you is a ritual abuse survivor, then you may have both human parts programmed as a ritual false Jesus and spirits in a false Jesus position to mock the true Jesus.

If there is a manifestation, I test the spirit. I will read quietly, under my breath, the litany of Jesus Christ and the litany of the Holy Spirit, to see if it provokes the demonic. I do this while the individual is distracted by one of my other team members. The goal is for the afflicted individual not to hear me read the prayer or see me. I will read it off my mobile phone like I am reading a text someone just sent me. Be coy about it. If there is a demon present, it will insist you stop what you are doing at once. Then I will tell him I am just reading a text on my phone, and return to what I am doing. The demon will insist again that you stop what you're doing. Where I will then proceed to read the litanies out loud. At this point, the demon may have already manifested and will want to leave the session. I will then pray out loud to bind the demon to the chair so it can't walk out of the prayer session. I have had situations where the demon manifested and got up in a crippled body and came after me to throw me out a window. I stood in my spiritual authority and bound the spirit to the chair. The person's body just dropped straight down into the chair and squirmed and wrestled. From the ministry perspective, it looked as if some had superglued the person's bottom to the chair. At the end of the session, this individual asked me what had happened because every muscle in his body was in pain. He could feel the after effects of the demon trying to break free of the prayer binding. I never hold people down during ministry or hold on to them. God is all about free will. If the demon is going to do harm to me, my prayer team, or the person, I will pray to bind the spirit. If the person continues to come after me, I know there is a human part in collusion with the demon. At that point, I ask the true Jesus inside the person to bring the Christian host back up. You must stay entirely in your realm of dominion; the spirits know you are operating under the authority of the heavenly Father. I operate as an ambassador and remind them of the laws they already know and must obey. He created the spirits for Him, by Him, and they are to serve Him. Always stand in your spiritual authority and your victory at the cross, no matter what magic show they put on. As a rule of thumb, I don't allow the magic shows in my session. These forbidden activities include witchcraft, manifestations, calling out to more demons, levitating, and even casting demons into you.

Remember, these are exorcism prayer sessions, which are face-to-face clashes with the forces of darkness. I have been through sessions where demons tried to possess me and also members of my team. We could feel the presence of spirits on our faces like something was trying to push its way into our souls. This situation is an example of why you already know you're walking in the covering and spiritual protection of God Most High.

In one incident when this happened, I told the demon if it was trying to possess me, the best way was through my eyes. The eyes are the lamp unto my soul. I ordered the demon to look me directly into my eyes. It wouldn't look into my eyes, so I ordered it one more time. I knew the Holy Spirit was giving me tactical information, a word of knowledge. The demon tried to look away, but it was bound and ordered to look into my eyes. The demon shuddered, and the person who was manifesting leaped from the seat cushions of the couch to the top of it trying to get away from me. It looked as if the demon wanted to scurry up the wall like a lizard, but the human body wasn't capable of that path of escape. The manifestation ended and the Christian core came up and asked me what the heck had just happened. The Holy Spirit in me was manifesting and looking back at the demon. We have lots of stories like these from ministry. I had one case recently when this happened again. It's freaky at first, but afterward, you know where you stand in these power encounters. You must stand your ground with the unseen real presence of God who is with you in battle. What I presented about the eyes is not a methodology on how to handle this situation. The methodology is to be listening to the indwelling God for what you need to be doing when situations like this arise. The sessions must always be operating in a state of peace under the direction of the Holy Spirit. Order and peace are sessions of the Holy Spirit, chaos and yelling are demonically controlled sessions.

Breaking Occult Vows

When working with former occult members and ritual abuse survivors, you will need to break off vows. Former occult members will need to bring their occult-familiar objects and books with them. You will first have the individual renounce the objects and their use and have them renounce Satan. They will then ask God for his forgiveness. Seems easy, right? Depending on how dark they went and what spirits they let into them, this could be a several-hour fight to renounce just one object. The demons attached to the objects will manifest and they will put on a crazy show of contortion, warfare, and possibly levitation. They will become exhausted in the battle because the demonic can't summon enough power to fight God. Even when they were in their full numbers and organized in heaven, they couldn't beat Him, so a lone demon and his band of brothers are no match for God. The whole point of the magic show is to weaken the person seeking freedom and to wear down the faith of the exorcism ministry team. When the battle is won, the occult item that was detached from the spirit needs to be burned. Time for a bonfire in an old barrel in the church parking lot. As the item burns, continue to pray for further liberation over the person and separation from the item in the pyre. Exorcism of a former occult member can take months to a year or years. Because the soul allowed the spirits in of his own free will, the demons think they have special legal grounds to return.

Breaking vows for an occult ritual abuse survivor takes a different approach. The demonic attachment to the human parts was created as a violation of an innocent child. A ministry member will intercede in the gap for the child to be liberated. The occult vows of death, blood, and blood sacrifices will be renounced, as well as any and all mocking rituals of the crucifixion of the Lord Jesus Christ. In the prayer, I pray to separate the human part from the demonic and for the true Jesus to keep the demons out of the prayer session. At this point, I am left with the traumatized and programmed child part, which is when I pray for the true Jesus to manifest and encounter the child. I pray for peace over the entire system so it is not in chaos or states of warfare. When the peace of Jesus Christ comes to the part, His spirit of truth comes in and breaks the lie of fear keeping the human child part in that dark bondage. The child must choose, of his own free will, to surrender to Jesus Christ and receive his healing. Again, these sessions take time as well, and there is no agenda or timeframe in healing. Jesus knows the time of the full healing. We just operate in sync with the will of the heavenly Father.

Protection, Covering, and Intercession

A ministry of exorcism requires a team. You never do this ministry alone. I can't imagine the horror and oppression a paranormal self-proclaimed exorcist goes through. This ignorant approach shares, as I've said before, the same mentality as swimming outside the protection of a shark cage with several large great white sharks nearby. You might survive, but chances are you won't, and you'll likely experience a very grisly and violent attack. If you survive, you will be scarred for life. This shark depiction is my metaphor for ghost hunting exorcists. Many have learned their lesson, but unfortunately, some still ghost hunt and think either Roman Catholic exorcists or I will come to their rescue. This is very bad tactical planning, especially when they expect God to save them. Remember, God loathes ghost hunting!

When involved in this level of spiritual warfare, you will constantly be under attack and oppression. To be operating as an exorcist, you will need a spiritual covering provided by God. His spiritual covering means that God has brought you into this fight and that He is protecting everything in your life from diabolic oppression. By diabolic oppression I mean attacks in the heavenly realms, as well as from the demonic. When I entered into deliverance ministry years ago, there were a lot of attacks going on at my house against my family, pets, children, and finances. We literally had our fire alarms going off every time my wife, Lisa, and I would intercede for a soul's liberation. A church we attended in our early days of ministry offered its spiritual covering, which provided an immediate reduction in oppression against us. However, through time, the church covering turned into human legalism and control. A lot of the warfare was coming from the fact that the ministry was expanding into exorcism. Warfare came in the form of mockery as well as a lack of understanding that God was orchestrating this ministry's development. It was a difficult time in my spiritual journey where the attacks were coming from all directions. I am sharing this for transparency, for those who think it would be cool to be an exorcist. The enemy hates this ministry, take this to heart.

I had long talks with Jesus as my frustration peaked and I felt like I was a volcano about to erupt. I had to move my ministry out from underneath the current church covering. There was also the issue that the church intercessor team wasn't prepared for the battles coming its way from having a ministry of exorcism under its roof. No one could prepare these intercessors for this level of warfare, and it wasn't fair to them to expose them to these attacks. The problem was, where would I move my ministry?

One day Jesus interrupted me in my long bantering diatribe and asked me who was Abraham, Jacob, Moses, and Elijah's covering? This conversation with God was a spiritual ah-ha moment for me. Sometime after that, God prophetically spoke to me in a dream, released me from the covering of the church and moved me into His spiritual protection.

Right when I thought the ministry was done, God opened the doors for me. God had a plan and under it I am spiritually covered. I now work with a counseling team that works with ritual abuse survivors. Our counselors, ministry team, and the healing souls we work with are under the attack of the occult constantly. Some survivors have healed enough to be on our intercessory prayer team. One key objective is that we protect the intercessors and filter what comes in on the request list. We only pray for our team and the souls we are working with in our sessions. The goal is not to overload the intercessors and to keep them focused on the theaters of battle. If someone sends us an e-mail to pray for their Aunt May who is sick, it won't reach the intercessors' list. We will have the request diverted to other ministries who pray for the sick. Likewise, when one of the souls we are working with asks for intercessory team prayer, we

188 • MICHAEL J. NORTON

ask the Holy Spirit for discernment to make sure this isn't the occult slipping prayer requests in to keep the team busy. The occult will do things like that to wear the intercessory team down or to look for holes in the electric fence of intercession. We don't reveal the makeup of the intercessory team or how we intercede, because that is tactical information we don't want out. If you develop an intercessory team, God will guide you, or you will be sent divine appointments of people who will assist you in setting this up. God is really incredible about doing this. As you can see, a ministry of exorcism requires a big team, from the ministry prayer team down to the intercessors. There is safety in numbers!

Finding an Exorcist

A final word of advice: if you are a former occult member or a ritual abuse survivor, don't try this prayer session on yourselves, nor have family members do it. There are some really good exorcists throughout the United States now. I highly respect the clergy of the Roman Catholic Church in this as well, if you require help. Too often we get in our heads this mindset or prejudice about certain denominations. The Roman Catholic exorcism clergy is great, and I know most of them. My advice is to seek help, because it won't come through your own efforts. There are also networks of ministry experts growing in both the Protestant and Roman Catholic denominations. If you go on the Internet seeking help, avoid the exorcists' web pages that give you the feeling you're reading about a shady television lawyer. If the first page you see is a non-Roman Catholic minister holding a crucifix at you, that may be a good sign to keep searching. Also, be aware that there is an order of exorcists that has nothing to do with the Roman Catholic International Association of Exorcists. Your best bet, if you can't find an exorcist, is to call your local Roman Catholic diocese. A false exorcist will make your matters worse, and then your situation will have compounded.

That's about as much information as I can cram into one chapter. I can easily write volumes on this, but this information provides an overview of what I call the Lutheran form of exorcism ministry, I hope you were able to see through examples that Lutheran exorcism ministry is just as effective as Roman Catholic exorcism ministry, even though there are differences in both forms of ministry. We share the same Holy Trinity and Scriptures. We just have two different approaches.

CHAPTER 15

Character of the Minister

In this chapter, I would like to provide my concluding thoughts on the ministries of deliverance, SRA prayer, and exorcism. Now that you understand what these ministries are, I would like to discuss an important matter that is critical to all of these offices of prayer, and that is the character of you, the minister.

I mentioned John Paul Jackson's Streams Ministries in a previous chapter (on hearing God). If you have taken the Stream's course on hearing God, the first section of the course emphasizes the character of the minister. Who are you in Christ? Can you operate in humility as one who is in a spiritual union with Him? No matter who Jesus puts before you in the prayer recipient's chair, you must operate in the compassion of Jesus Christ. You may immediately observe that the person requesting help is not demonized but merely not seeing the large plank sticking out of his eye.

The job of the minister is to convey the truth of what the indwelling Jesus is showing and what the Holy Spirit is revealing in the session. Maturity is everything, and you must operate in your God-given wisdom. You may pray for someone who has a convincing story that they're being demonized. During the prayer session with this individual, nothing spiritual happens and you feel no demonic presence. What do you do? You tell them the truth! You felt nothing. The Holy Spirit may also give you the revelation that there is nothing going on here. You go with what the

Holy Spirit is revealing to you. I have witnessed far too many deliverance sessions where the ministers felt they were inadequate and sensed nothing because other big name deliverance ministers saw a demon on this person. So the lesser-known deliverance ministers lie about how they saw demons attached to the person. This false seeing is giving into pride and demonic lies. And it happens far too many times, more than I care to admit. If you see or feel no presence, then tell the person the truth. The other deliverance ministers may have been lying to this person out of their own insecurities as well. You may be the first minister delivering an ounce of truth to the situation: that there are no demons and this person just needs to own his irresponsible behaviors. I have spent a lot of time in my counseling sessions undoing bad deliverance ministry!

A Case of Dealing with Bad Character in Ministry

I recently worked with a young woman, Shannon, who was frustrated with deliverance ministers not being able to help her. Shannon contacted me about her battle with a spiritual attachment she was experiencing. Based on the frustrated tone of Shannon's voice, I agreed to meet with her. I called in my prayer team member, Adrienne, and we set up a time to meet with Shannon for that upcoming weekend.

On Saturday evening, we met at the counseling office to evaluate what was going on with Shannon. As we sat for our initial "meet and greet," Shannon proceeded to tell us some crazy stories of her prior deliverance sessions. One of the craziest stories, which I am sharing here, reflects on the character of the minister.

Shannon shared with us a story about a minister that titled herself as a prophetess but also did some deliverance ministry on the side. Shannon was a beautician, and one day the prophetess approached her and delivered this unusual and demanding request.

"I have prayed for you so many times, and you need to do my nails."

Shannon thought it was odd but agreed, since the woman did pray for her quite a bit, and set up the nail appointment.

When the day came for the prophetess to come in, Shannon received a phone call notifying her of the appointment cancellation. The reason for the cancellation was that the prophetess didn't want her prophetic anointing tainted by Shannon's oppressed hands touching her. Can you see the character flaws in the prophetess? Where is the compassion of Jesus? The prophetess in Shannon's story reminded me of Jesus's parable of the Pharisee and the tax collector. The Pharisee stood and was praying this to himself: "God, I thank You that I am not like other people: swindlers, unjust, adulterers, or even like this tax collector" (Luke 10:11).

Now, here is what Adrienne and I discovered in our session with Shannon. In front of us was this incredibly unpolished diamond of God, a young Christian who had the ability to connect with God and hear His voice. She knew the voice of her Shepherd, and she willfully followed Him. With this realization, Adrienne and I had to discern why the spirits were focused on attacking Shannon. Shannon had done some tarot card reading in the past, but she had renounced and repented of the sinful behavior. When Adrienne and I prayed with Shannon, there were no demonic manifestations. I asked Shannon if we saw the same results as other ministers. She said yes, but the other deliverance ministers said they could see the demons around her. Adrienne and I saw nothing! Shannon mentioned that after the first deliverances, the spirits left her but were still oppressing her externally. They would touch her or poke her to annoy her on occasion. Since the spirits did not have any access to inside her body, Adrienne and I had the revelation that Shannon was dealing with some oppression that was allowed by God to teach her how to use spiritual warfare. As we shared this with Shannon, it resonated with her, because she felt she was called into deliverance ministry. However, her calling inspirations felt dashed because she was always knocked down by poorly equipped deliverance ministers. Adrienne and I conveyed to Shannon that God doesn't wait for people to be perfectly healed before He starts using them in ministry. A huge weight was lifted off Shannon's heart in knowing that God wasn't benching her for seeking her freedom. In this session, Shannon was delivered from bad deliverance ministry and ministers whose character didn't align with helping others heal. I followed up with Shannon sometime later, and she said she was doing great now that she had the understanding of what was going on with her spiritually.

Spiritual Maturity and Faith

Fear is the biggest factor for new ministers when they go to prayer sessions. The enemy uses the fear of being unprepared to derail many new deliverance ministries. I remember early on in my ministry days: I felt like a lawyer prepared for battle. I got my Scriptures ready, grabbed the books with the best curse-breaking prayers, and off I went to the prayer ministry session. However, none of this prep was ever of any use. God leads the deliverance session, and He's the one who does all the preparation. I travel a lot lighter now. I only bring a Bible to the sessions. And I don't prepare at all. All the real preparation is done during the week with the time I spend one-on-one with Jesus. Would you believe there is very little warfare prayer during my one-on-one time? My time is focused on being in the company of Jesus in His presence. Meditation on the "Our Father" (The Lord's Prayer) in Matthew 6 is sufficient for spiritual warfare prep. Jesus knows what I am facing. Mental prayer is everything. Mental prayer is simply dialogues with Jesus in my heart and soul. When I hear God during battle, it is as sublime as it is during mental prayer. I don't have crazy visions or hear the voice of God thundering in my soul. It is very gentle and quiet. God is the same in mental prayer as He is in warfare. This requires a maturity in your walk in faith that Jesus will always do something (and it's usually beyond our comprehension) for the situation we are in.

Character and Identity in Christ During Battle

Recently, I was called by one of my ritual abuse survivor friends, Janice, to assist her with an issue she was dealing with from one of her parts. An occult loyal part felt it necessary to open a spiritual portal in her bedroom. I responded to the call and went out to shut down the open portal. Now, as a class exercise, find how to close one of these in one of the popular deliverance books on the market. A little hint: it's not in any of them!

That's why these books are useless in battle, and you must have faith and an interior life to hear the indwelling Jesus Christ.

When I arrived at the home, my friend Janice took me to her room where she said one of her parts had opened the portal. I asked Janice to wait in the other room for me. I wanted to walk the room and get a feel for what was happening in the room. I walked around the room, and in the dead center of her room, there was this weird chill. It was weird in the nature that it was only present at that location, and the chill had a slight motion to it. It was like someone put a tiny fan in the floor, and there was a small gentle cyclone stirring the air. This was tangible in the physical reality. I determined I had located the portal in the room. Janice and the woman caring for her entered the room and saw where I was standing with a strange look of bewilderment on my face. Janice said, "It didn't take you long to find it."

I told her, "This is crazy stuff!"

Janice friend commented. "Can you feel the whirlwind?"

I just nodded in affirmation.

At that moment, as I stood in the portal, I could hear the voice of Jesus telling me to deliver a message to the part that was opening the portal to the occult. Jesus gave me a specific name of the spirit, which, for obvious reasons, I won't repeat. I walked over and looked Janice in the eyes to speak to her parts, and I told her the Lord Jesus Christ had ordered the spirit (name withheld) to stand down. And that Mike (yes, this came out in the third person, awkward) was going to shut the portal down. No one was to retaliate.

Keep in mind this is not a recipe to shut down portals; I want to give you a glimpse of how Jesus rolls in warfare. I didn't have any anointing oil, so I'd brought some olive oil which I blessed on the spot. I used the olive oil and stood in the portal and prayed it closed, in the name of Jesus Christ. I sealed the floor with the lettering JHS, written with my finger in anointing oil: Latin for Jesus Hominum Salvator, Jesus is the Savior of mankind. Jesus had me write it in Latin so traversing spirits would see it. Again, I was not using a recipe or process for this. It was what I was instructed to do by the indwelling Jesus. The portal was closed, and at that moment, one of the occult parts that had created the portal switched in. Janice ran and locked herself in the bathroom, and we had to minister to the part from the opposite side of the locked bathroom door. Jesus's demonstration of having the ability to close occult portals was a power encounter. The part surrendered to Jesus a few hours later and was healed.

As you can see, there is no rhyme, reason, or way to prepare for battle other than to show up and work with Jesus. The most important thing is your ability to connect with God. That takes a lot of work in prayer with Jesus Christ. You must walk in faith, and you must hear God. You will notice in these examples that I didn't bind the spirit of Jezebel, or any other spirit most deliverance ministers rattle off during ministry. That's not operating with God but operating on your own knowledge and pride. God trains you in baby steps, and He raises you up. You must have the spiritual maturity and faith to step into the unknown. I never have a plan for battle, I just show up and see what Jesus is going to do. Things go really smoothly and I don't have a lot of worries about warfare. Don't get me wrong; we still go through intense battles, I just don't worry about the warfare. Jesus orchestrates the battle and all the spirits submit to Him. Just follow along with what Jesus is doing and ask Him for revelation. He doesn't usually reveal all of His plans until the end of the battle. In prayer, I never presume to direct Jesus in warfare, only to fall into alignment with His will.

Seeing Demons

During ministry, you may or may not see a demonic spirit. If you are to see a demonic spirit in its true form, it is through the grace of God. It seems to be a deliverance ministry fad where ministers tell prayer recipients they see demons on them. I am always skeptical of these stories, but I think I know why this is prevalent in these days in ministry.

My first reason has to do with poorly equipped ministers. If you are going to use prophetic ministry, you must understand that if you see a picture of a demon in your mind, do not convey that to the prayer recipient. Remember, we perceive what the Holy Spirit is telling us in the eye of the soul. Imagery can be one of three sources: God, our souls, or other messengers. You must test the spirit, and discern first the source you are receiving from. I believe that nine times out of ten, new ministers get caught up in the moment and believe they see a demon. Then they convey it to the person they are praying for with no intention of malice. However, the recipient is really caught off guard by the revelation, which is not true. It came from the prayer minister's soul. I have already mentioned not doing this when working with DID souls. They are literally freaked out by revelation and have a hard time shaking it off themselves. Don't do this to them unless you plan to hold their hand for the next decade in counseling because they can't shake what you told them.

I worked with one ritual abuse survivor, Jamie, who's constantly putting herself into a spin and slowing down her healing whenever she seeks deliverance ministry. She becomes impatient with me because I tell her there are no demons on her. I can discern that, and I can feel the presence of demons. So she'll go out for a second opinion from an ill-equipped deliverance minister, and because he doesn't understand DID, he tells her there are dark demons all over her. And she won't shake it off. I will spend the next session spinning wheels in the mud convincing Jamie she doesn't have demons. I am at the point where I would really like to drag ill-equipped deliverance ministers who say this into our counseling sessions and show them the damage they do to people. If you can't discern demons, don't tell people they have demons on them! In my ministry, I never tell people if I see any spirits. That is tactical information I don't share.

Another reason a minister does this is to falsely promote his ministry. It is a lie that his ministry in moving in the power of the Holy Spirit. I have probably been through a thousand deliverance sessions at the time of this writing. Very seldom have I seen demons. Only through the grace of God are they revealed, and only when He feels like He wants to reveal the unseen spirit realm. Some minsters I have known who claimed to consistently see demons or hear from angels at a supernatural level, went off the deep end. The most common form of spiritual discernment is the feeling you get in your body of the presence of a manifestation. These were ministers who ignored their humility, sought pride and power, and seriously needed to check their character.

Interior Life, Tribulations, and Rest

If there are no good books out there on this ministry, then where should one start if he feels drafted into this? It boils down to who you are in Christ and your character in Him. Learn everything you can about the Word of God without becoming doctrinal. The laws in Leviticus and Deuteronomy are equally as important as the four Gospels. Most of the occult is called out in the Mosaic laws. Learn God's laws, especially those pertaining to spirituality. Above all, develop a deep prayer life with Jesus Christ. It doesn't have to be perfect. We're talking about quality time with Him. Learn to hear His voice under all conditions. Learn how He speaks to you, and learn how your body discerns spirits.

Never try to imitate what you see other deliverance ministers doing. If God has drafted you into this, you are going to be a masterpiece for a specific type of warfare. What type of warfare? It's usually what God reveals to you. Let Him train you. Let the Holy Spirit raise you up to your own unique ministry. If you're drafted, God will take you through seasons of tribulations to sift you and expose you to things He wants you to understand. This all comes about through the sanctification of your soul. Some of these tribulations you will endure might seem more overwhelming, and you won't know how to find the strength to take on more warfare. That's God's way of stretching you for ministry. You may be going through a sifting that feels like it's ripping you apart, and yet you will have to find the strength to pray for others (plural) and come alongside them in warfare. God gives you breaks too, and you must recognize those as mini-sabbaticals to rest physically and spiritually. I find that when God puts me into a small time of rest, I get the worst requests. They're stirred by the enemy to interrupt my rejuvenation time in Jesus. I don't take on battles during my time of rest. When I tell people I can't help them, or that I am at my maximum number of cases I can handle, they take it as an offense. Do not let people overload you with their oppression when asking for help. You're not Jesus, and only He can heal people. I found the people who literally push you for help or seem extremely off in their Christian walk are not allowing Jesus to help them in the first place. Don't let people pressure you into ministry when Jesus is telling to you to rest. Jesus cares first and foremost about the minister and not the ministry.

CHAPTER 16

Closing Thoughts

I can devote volumes to this subject matter, and I most likely will in future writings. But this information you have in your hands should be sufficient to help launch or grow you in some of the things you have been experiencing in ministry. This ministry is not about demons or proving the existence of the spirit realm. It is all about bringing pastoral care for afflicted souls through the compassion and healing of Jesus Christ. Always give the afflicted souls the truth, no matter if they want to believe it or not. People would rather believe they have a demonic affliction than address the white elephant in the room, such as a meth addiction or lack of responsibility for their ungodly behaviors. When you call these behaviors out, do so with the utmost respect to their condition and their hearts. You must bring their souls spiritual direction and truth. They may need an exorcism or they may need a drug rehab program such as Teen Challenge. I find myself frequently speaking truth that goes against the words a popular deliverance minister or charismatic prophetic speaker has spoken over a person. People get it wrong; we're human. When I get revelations about a person, many times other people on my prayer team are receiving the same information. There are checks and balances in the ministry. This is why I spend time with people to get a feel for who they are, what their walk with Christ is like, and what behaviors they're not willing to address and crucify. If the situation is extremely difficult,

201

you will get better revelation in prayer than you will from a deliverance book. You may get answers right away in prayer, or information may be slowly released to you as Jesus brings healing. This goes back to spiritual direction, who you are in Christ, and your connection with God. God will release you into and direct all your battles. Just be a part of what He is doing in these battles.

Blessings to you in your ministry to heal souls!

God bless,

Michael

Protection Prayers

*Note: used for ministry dealing with the occult

True Lord Jesus, born through your virgin mother, Mary; Jesus, who led a sinless, holy life. Jesus, you followed the will of your heavenly Father to the cross and were the only true sacrifice for mankind's sin. Jesus, you died on the cross and were resurrected from the grave through the power of the Holy Spirit. It is to you and you alone we speak to in this prayer session. Jesus, we ask you to push out all false representations of you in this session.

Jesus you are the king of heaven and all of heaven belongs to you. If any attacks or assignments of retribution are coming from your heavenly realm, we ask that you protect us and cloak us from the dark angelic realm. Please cut off all communication, powers, and programming being used against us in this ministry session that is originating out of our spiritual authority dominion.

We bind demonic spirits in our dominion and forbid them from calling out to higher spirits.

Jesus protect our families, ministries, properties, finances, and give us complete protective covering from the enemy.

We ask these things in your precious name, Jesus Christ.

Amen.

Litany of Holy Name of Jesus Christ

*Note: Litany prayers are for deliverance and exorcism prayer ministry only. Do not use in ritual abuse prayer ministry.

Lord, have mercy on us.[1]
Christ, have mercy on us.
Lord, have mercy on us.
Father all powerful, have mercy on us
Jesus, Eternal Son of the Father, Redeemer of the world,
save us.
Spirit of the Father and the Son, boundless life of both,
sanctify us.
Holy Trinity, hear us

Holy Ghost, Who proceedest from the Father and the Son, enter our hearts.
Holy Ghost, Who art equal to the Father and the Son, enter our hearts.

Promise of God the Father, have mercy on us.
Ray of heavenly light, have mercy on us

---

1 http://www.catholic.org/prayers/prayer.php?p=463

Author of all good, have mercy on us
Source of heavenly water, have mercy on us
Consuming fire, have mercy on us
Ardent charity, have mercy on us
Spiritual unction, have mercy on us
Spirit of love and truth, have mercy on us
Spirit of wisdom and understanding, have mercy on us
Spirit of counsel and fortitude, have mercy on us
Spirit of knowledge and piety, have mercy on us
Spirit of the fear of the Lord, have mercy on us
Spirit of grace and prayer, have mercy on us
Spirit of peace and meekness, have mercy on us
Spirit of modesty and innocence, have mercy on us
Holy Ghost, the Comforter, have mercy on us
Holy Ghost, the Sanctifier, have mercy on us
Holy Ghost, Who governest the Church, have mercy on us
Gift of God, the Most High, have mercy on us
Spirit Who fillest the universe, have mercy on us
Spirit of the adoption of the children of God, have mercy on us

Holy Ghost, inspire us with horror of sin.
Holy Ghost, come and renew the face of the earth.
Holy Ghost, shed Thy light in our souls.
Holy Ghost, engrave Thy law in our hearts
Holy Ghost, inflame us with the flame of Thy love.
Holy Ghost, open to us the treasures of Thy graces
Holy Ghost, teach us to pray well.
Holy Ghost, enlighten us with Thy heavenly inspirations.
Holy Ghost, lead us in the way of salvation
Holy Ghost, grant us the only necessary knowledge.
Holy Ghost, inspire in us the practice of good.
Holy Ghost, grant us the merits of all virtues.
Holy Ghost, make us persevere in justice.
Holy Ghost, be Thou our everlasting reward.

Lamb of God, Who takest away the sins of the world, Send us Thy Holy Ghost.

Lamb of God, Who takest away the sins of the world, pour down into our souls the gifts of the Holy Ghost.

Lamb of God, Who takest away the sins of the world, grant us the Spirit of wisdom and piety.

Come, Holy Ghost! Fill the hearts of Thy faithful, And enkindle in them the fire of Thy love.

Let Us Pray
Grant, O merciful Father, that Thy Divine Spirit may enlighten, inflame and purify us, that He may penetrate us with His heavenly dew and make us fruitful in good works, through Our Lord Jesus Christ, Thy Son, Who with Thee, in the unity of the same Spirit, liveth and reigneth forever and ever. Amen

Litany of the Passion

*Note: Litany prayers are for deliverance and exorcism prayer ministry only. Do not use in ritual abuse prayer ministry.

Lord, have mercy[1]
Christ, have mercy
Lord, have mercy
Christ, hear us.
Christ, graciously hear us.
God the Father of heaven,
Have mercy on us.

God the Son, Redeemer of the world,
Have mercy on us.
God the Holy Spirit,
Have mercy on us.
Holy Trinity, one God,
Have mercy on us.
Jesus, the eternal Wisdom,
Have mercy on us.
Jesus, conversing with men,

---

1 http://www.catholic.org/prayers/prayer.php?p=466

Have mercy on us.

Jesus, hated by the world,

Have mercy on us.

Jesus, sold for thirty pieces of silver,

Have mercy on us.

Jesus, prostrate in prayer,

Have mercy on us.

Jesus, strengthened by an angel,

Have mercy on us.

Jesus, agonizing in a bloody sweat,

Have mercy on us.

Jesus, betrayed by Judas with a kiss,

Have mercy on us.

Jesus, bound by the soldiers,

Have mercy on us.

Jesus, forsaken by your disciples,

Have mercy on us.

Jesus, before Annas and Caiaphas,

Have mercy on us.

Jesus, struck by a servant on the face,

Have mercy on us.

Jesus, accused by false witnesses,

Have mercy on us.

Jesus, declared worthy of death,

Have mercy on us.

Jesus, spit upon in the face,

Have mercy on us.

Jesus, blindfolded,

Have mercy on us.

Jesus, smitten on the cheek,

Have mercy on us.

Jesus, thrice denied by Peter,

Have mercy on us.

Jesus, delivered up to Pilate,

Have mercy on us.

Jesus, despised and mocked by Herod,

Have mercy on us.

Jesus, clothed in a white garment,

Have mercy on us.

Jesus, rejected for Barabbas,

Have mercy on us.

Jesus, torn by sources,

Have mercy on us.

Jesus, bruised for our sins,

Have mercy on us.

Jesus, regarded as a leper,

Have mercy on us.

Jesus, covered with a purple robe,

Have mercy on us.

Jesus, crowned with thorns,

Have mercy on us.

Jesus, struck with a reed,

Have mercy on us.

Jesus, demanded for crucifixion,

Have mercy on us.

Jesus, condemned to death,

Have mercy on us.

Jesus, given up to your enemies,

Have mercy on us.

Jesus, laden with the Cross,

Have mercy on us.

Jesus, led as a lamb to the slaughter,

Have mercy on us.

Jesus, stripped of your garments,

Have mercy on us.

Jesus, fastened with nails to the Cross,

Have mercy on us.

Jesus, wounded for our iniquities,

Have mercy on us.

Jesus, praying for your murderers,

Have mercy on us.

Jesus, reputed with the wicked,

Have mercy on us.

Jesus, blasphemed on the Cross,

Have mercy on us.

Jesus, reviled by the malefactor,

Have mercy on us.

Jesus, giving Paradise to the thief,

Have mercy on us.

Jesus, commending Saint John to your Mother as her son,

Have mercy on us.

Jesus, forsaken by your Father,

Have mercy on us.

Jesus, given fall and vinegar to drink,

Have mercy on us.

Jesus, testifying that all things written concerning you were accomplished

Have mercy on us.

Jesus, commending your spirit into the hands of your Father,

Have mercy on us.

Jesus, obedient even unto death,

Have mercy on us.

Jesus, pierced with a lance,

Have mercy on us.

Jesus, made a propitiation for us,

Have mercy on us.

Jesus, taken down from the Cross,

Have mercy on us.

Jesus, laid in a sepulcher,

Have mercy on us.

Jesus, rising gloriously from the dead,

Have mercy on us.

Jesus, ascending into heaven,

Have mercy on us.
Jesus, our Advocate with the Father,
Have mercy on us.
Jesus, sending down the Holy Spirit,
Have mercy on us.
Jesus, exalting your Mother,
Have mercy on us.
Jesus, who shall come to judge the living and the dead,
Have mercy on us.

Be merciful,
spare us, O Lord.
Be merciful,
graciously hear us, O Lord.

From all evil,
deliver us, O Jesus.
From all sin,
deliver us, O Jesus.
From anger, hatred, and every evil will,
deliver us, O Jesus.
From war, famine, and pestilence,
deliver us, O Jesus.
From all dangers of mind and body,
deliver us, O Jesus.
From everlasting death,
deliver us, O Jesus.
Through your most pure conception,
deliver us, O Jesus.
Through your miraculous nativity,
deliver us, O Jesus.
Through your humble circumcision,
deliver us, O Jesus.
Through your baptism and fasting,

deliver us, O Jesus.

Through your labors and watchings,

deliver us, O Jesus.

Through your cruel scourging and crowning,

deliver us, O Jesus.

Through your thirst, and tears, and nakedness,

deliver us, O Jesus.

Through your precious death and Cross,

deliver us, O Jesus.

Through your glorious resurrection and ascension,

deliver us, O Jesus.

Through your sending forth the Holy Spirit, the Paraclete,

deliver us, O Jesus.

On the day of judgment, we sinners,

we beseech you, hear us.

That you would spare us,

we beseech you, hear us.

That you would pardon us,

we beseech you, hear us.

That you would bring us to true penance,

we beseech you, hear us.

That you would pour into our hearts the grace of the Holy Spirit,

we beseech you, hear us.

That you would defend and propagate your Church,

we beseech you, hear us.

That you would preserve and increase all societies assembled in your holy Name,

we beseech you, hear us.

That you would bestow upon us true peace, humility, and charity,

we beseech you, hear us.

That you would give us perseverance in grace and in your holy service,

we beseech you, hear us.

That you would deliver us from unclean thoughts, the temptations of the devil, and everlasting damnation,
we beseech you, hear us.
That you would unite us to the company of your Saints,
we beseech you, hear us.
That you would graciously hear us,
we beseech you, hear us.

Lamb of God, you take away the sins of the world;
spare us, O Lord.
Lamb of God, you take away the sins of the world;
graciously hear us, O Lord.
Lamb of God, you take away the sins of the world;
have mercy on us.
Christ hear us.
Christ, graciously hear us.
Lord, have mercy.
Christ, have mercy.
Lord, have mercy.

We adore you, O Christ, and we bless you, because by your holy Cross you have redeemed the world.

Litany of the Cross

*Note: Litany prayers are for deliverance and exorcism prayer ministry only. Do not use in ritual abuse prayer ministry.

The cross is the hope of Christians[2]
the cross is the resurrection of the dead
the cross is the way of the lost
the cross is the savior of the lost
the cross is the staff of the lame
the cross is the guide of the blind
the cross is the strength of the weak
the cross is the doctor of the sick
the cross is the aim of the priests
the cross is the hope of the hopeless
the cross is the freedom of the slaves
the cross is the power of the kings
the cross is the water of the seeds
the cross is the consolation of the bondsmen
the cross is the source of those who seek water
the cross is the cloth of the naked.
We thank you, Father, for the cross

---

2 http://www.catholic.org/prayers/prayer.php?p=462

91840732R00130

Made in the USA
Lexington, KY
26 June 2018